OCCASIONAL PAPER 171

Monetary Policy in Dollarized Economies

By a Staff Team led by
Tomás J.T. Baliño, Adam Bennett, and Eduardo Borensztein

and comprising
Andrew Berg
Zhaohui Chen
Alain Ize
David O. Robinson
Abebe Aemro Selassie
Lorena Zamalloa

INTERNATIONAL MONETARY FUND
Washington DC

Production: IMF Graphics Section
Figures: In-Ok Yoon
Typesetting: Alicia Etchebarne-Bourdin and Julio R. Prego

Library of Congress Cataloging-in-Publication Data

Monetary policy in dollarized economies / Tomás Baliño, Adam Bennett, and Eduardo Borensztein.
    p.   cm.—(Occasional paper; 171)
   ISBN 1-55775-757-7 (paper)
    1. Monetary policy—Developing countries. 2. Foreign exchange—Developing countries. 3. Dollar, American. I. Bennett, Adam. II. Borensztein, Eduardo. III. Title. IV. Series: Occasional paper (International Monetary Fund); no. 171.

HG1496.B345   1999
332.4'91724—dc21
                                     98-43299
                                          CIP

Price: US$18.00
(US$15.00 to full-time faculty members and
students at universities and colleges)

Please send orders to:
International Monetary Fund, Publication Services
700 19th Street, N.W., Washington, D.C. 20431, U.S.A.
Tel.: (202) 623-7430   Telefax: (202) 623-7201
E-mail: publications@imf.org
Internet: http://www.imf.org

recycled paper

Contents

The following symbols have been used throughout this paper:

. . .   to indicate that data are not available;

—   to indicate that the figure is zero or less than half the final digit shown, or that the item does not exist;

–   between years or months (for example, 1994–95 or January–June) to indicate the years or months covered, including the beginning and ending years or months;

/   between years (for example, 1994/95) to indicate a crop or fiscal (financial) year.

"Billion" means a thousand million.

Minor discrepancies between constituent figures and totals are due to rounding.

The term "country," as used in this paper, does not in all cases refer to a territorial entity that is a state as understood by international law and practice; the term also covers some territorial entities that are not states, but for which statistical data are maintained and provided internationally on a separate and independent basis.

Abbreviations

CBD	Cross-border deposits
CMIR	Currency and Monetary Instruments Reports
DCC	Dollar currency in circulation
FCD	Foreign currency deposits
FCL	Foreign currency loans
FCR	Foreign currency reserves (required for FCD)
LCD	Local currency deposits
NDA	Net domestic assets
NFA	Net foreign assets
NIR	Net international reserves
RR	Reserve requirements

Preface

Dollarization, which is a common feature in many countries, particularly developing countries and countries in transition, has important economic implications. This Occasional Paper analyses the costs and benefits of dollarization and explores its prudential and monetary policy implications. In particular, the paper reviews dollarization trends; explores the various monetary and exchange rate policy strategies that may be pursued in the presence of dollarization; and examines the implications of dollarization for the conduct of monetary policy, the issue of prudential norms and regulations, and the design of IMF programs. The paper also considers the effectiveness and drawbacks of measures to limit dollarization.

The authors thank Guillermo Calvo and Peter Garber, who provided comments on early versions of the paper, as well as many colleagues at the IMF but especially Paul Masson, Ratna Sahay, and Tessa van der Willigen, and members of the Executive Board for valuable comments and a stimulating Board seminar discussion in January 1998.

Kiran Sastry and Manzoor Gill provided research assistance, and Magally Bernal, Usha David, Jacqueline Greene, Sylvia Palazzo, and Bogna Jezierska secretarial assistance. James McEuen of the External Relations Department edited the paper for publication and coordinated production.

The views expressed here are the sole responsibility of the authors and do not necessarily represent the opinions of the Executive Board of the IMF or other members of the IMF staff.

I Overview

Dollarization, the holding by residents of a significant share of their assets in the form of foreign-currency-denominated assets, is a common feature of developing countries and transition economies and is thereby typical—to a greater or lesser extent—of many countries that have IMF-supported adjustment programs.[1] Of those countries that have had arrangements with the IMF at one time or another during the past ten years, at least half are dollarized, and a significant number are highly dollarized (Table 1).[2] This paper explores the general question of the costs and benefits of dollarization for a country's economy. In addition, it examines the issues that dollarization poses for the formulation and conduct of monetary policy, as well as for IMF program design.[3]

The paper focuses on dollarization of the monetary sector, and in particular on holdings by residents of foreign currency deposits (FCD) and, where data are available, of foreign currency cash. The paper recognizes, however, that dollarization of monetary assets often is part of a larger process of financial market integration. For example, dollarization in the loan portfolio of banks is an important phenomenon, and the paper touches on this too. Cross-border deposits (bank deposits of residents in foreign countries) also play an important role as close substitutes for domestic FCD. The paper explores the various monetary policy strategies that may be pursued in the presence of dollarization, considers the implications of dollarization for the practical application and instruments of monetary policy, and examines the manner in which dollarization has influenced the design of IMF programs. The paper's conclusions are as follows.

- The benefits of dollarization include closer integration with international markets, exposure to competition from these markets, and the availability of a more complete range of assets for domestic investors. In countries in which inflationary experience has destroyed confidence in the local currency, dollarization can sometimes help to remonetize the economy, restore local intermediation, and reverse capital flight. The costs of dollarization include the loss of seignorage and a potential for greater fragility of the banking system. Such fragilities can limit the policy options available to the authorities, as well as put an additional burden on the central bank as lender of last resort.

- Dollarization can complicate the choice of intermediate targets of monetary policy by introducing a foreign currency component into the money supply. The suitability of a target that includes, or excludes, foreign currency depends on the target's relationship with output and prices, and this is essentially an empirical matter. It is possible, however, that no reliable aggregate can be found. This problem, which is by no means confined to dollarized economies, brings into question the policy of monetary targeting as opposed to, for example, relying on a wider set of indicators. Although this issue is beyond the scope of this paper, there are good reasons to believe that dollar-denominated assets should play some role among the set of relevant indicators for monetary policy under any alternative approach.

- While the general considerations regarding the choice of exchange rate system also apply to dollarized economies, the prevalence of currency substitution (the use of foreign-currency-denominated assets for transactions) tends to strengthen the case for a fixed-rate system. Such an exchange rate arrangement would protect the economy from the effects of potentially excessive exchange rate and money market volatility. When attempting stabilization from hyperinflation, in particular, a fixed exchange rate can be an effective instrument in highly dollarized

---

[1]The foreign currency is usually, but not always, the U.S. dollar. The term "dollarization" serves as a shorthand in this paper for the use of any foreign currency.

[2]Of the 99 countries that have had IMF arrangements since 1986, 52 reported data on foreign currency deposits (FCD) to the IMF. In those countries reporting data, the median level of FCD over broad money in 1995 was 21.8 percent.

[3]Several of the issues discussed in this paper (for example, foreign currency risks) arise also in other foreign exchange operations, even if the economy is not dollarized in the sense discussed above.

Table 1. Reported Ratios of Foreign Currency Deposits (FCD) Broad Money in Countries with IMF Arrangements Since 1986

Country	1990	1991	1992	1993	1994	1995
Highly dollarized economies (FCD/broad money > 30 percent) (18)[1]						
Argentina	**34.2**	**35.1**	**37.1**	**40.4**	**43.2**	**43.9**
Azerbaijan	...	...	...	14.8	58.9	50.3
Belarus[2]	...	...	...	40.6	54.3	30.7
Bolivia	**70.8**	**76.8**	**80.8**	**83.9**	**81.9**	**82.3**
Cambodia	...	...	**26.3**	**38.8**	**51.8**	**56.4**
Costa Rica	...	37.7	31.9	29.5	30.3	31.0
Croatia	...	...	...	53.8	50.2	57.4
Georgia	...	...	...	...	80.1	30.8
Guinea-Bissau	41.5	34.7	31.6	30.9	31.1	31.2
Lao P. D. R.	**42.0**	**39.4**	**36.8**	**41.4**	**34.4**	**35.6**
Latvia	...	...	...	27.2	27.5	31.1
Mozambique[3]	...	11.8	16.7	23.2	25.3	32.6
Nicaragua	...	28.7	37.4	45.6	48.6	54.5
Peru	...	**59.9**	**65.0**	**70.2**	**64.2**	**64.0**
São Tomé and Príncipe	...	...	...	...	38.3	31.9
Tajikistan	...	...	...	...	...	33.7
Turkey	**23.2**	**29.7**	**33.7**	**37.9**	**45.8**	**46.1**
Uruguay	**80.1**	**78.5**	**76.2**	**73.3**	**74.1**	**76.1**
Median	41.7	36.4	36.8	40.4	48.6	39.7
Average	48.6	43.3	43.0	43.4	49.4	45.5
Moderately dollarized economies (FCD/broad money < 30 percent) (34)[1]						
Albania	2.1	1.3	23.8	20.4	18.5	...
Armenia	...	...	...	...	41.6	20.4
Bulgaria	12.0	33.4	23.4	20.3	32.6	28.4
Czech Republic[3]	...	...	...	...	7.2	5.9
Dominica	...	3.0	3.9	3.5	2.5	1.5
Ecuador	...	...	...	2.8	5.4	...
Egypt	...	50.7	37.3	26.7	23.4	25.1
El Salvador	...	1.4	1.0	0.9	0.6	1.7
Estonia	...	...	**23.0**	**3.8**	**9.9**	**11.4**
Guinea[4]	...	6.5	6.9	10.0	9.4	9.6
Honduras	...	3.1	5.1	7.6	11.4	13.0
Hungary	**12.2**	**16.5**	**14.3**	**18.7**	**20.4**	**26.6**
Jamaica	...	...	21.3	19.5	28.1	25.0
Jordan	**12.5**	**13.0**	**12.8**	**11.5**	**12.2**	**15.2**
Lithuania	...	...	...	...	27.0	25.9
Macedonia, FYR	...	...	...	...	...	18.1
Malawi	...	...	...	...	10.6	8.0
Mexico[2]	...	3.9	4.1	3.6	6.2	7.2
Moldova[3]	...	...	...	...	10.3	11.0
Mongolia	...	...	7.5	33.0	19.5	20.5
Pakistan[5]	**2.6**	**8.9**	**11.9**	**13.9**	**13.6**	...
Philippines	17.4	18.0	21.0	22.6	20.9	21.5
Poland	**31.4**	**24.7**	**24.8**	**28.8**	**28.5**	**20.4**
Romania	...	3.9	17.9	29.0	22.1	21.7
Russia	...	...	...	29.5	28.8	20.6
Sierra Leone	...	...	...	3.3	7.8	16.5
Slovak Republic	...	...	...	11.5	13.0	11.1
Trinidad and Tobago	...	...	...	6.9	12.6	13.6
Uganda	12.0	10.5	11.5	15.7	13.3	13.5
Ukraine	...	...	...	19.4	32.0	26.9

Table I *(concluded)*

Country	1990	1991	1992	1993	1994	1995
Uzbekistan[2]	...	...	20.1	5.1	22.5	15.5
Vietnam	...	...	25.9	20.9	20.4	19.7
Yemen		10.8	12.1	19.7	20.7	20.9
Zambia	...	...	...	...	8.1	16.2
Median	12.1	9.7	14.3	15.7	13.6	16.5
Average	12.8	13.3	15.9	15.0	17.2	16.4
Memorandum						
Selected industrial countries						
Greece	11.5	13.2	14.8	16.6	15.0	21.6
Netherlands	8.7	7.2	7.2	3.9	4.7	4.4
United Kingdom	11.4	7.7	10.5	10.9	12.6	15.4

Sources: IMF, IMF Staff Country Reports and *International Financial Statistics (IFS)*.
[1]Classification based on observations for 1995; countries in bold are those selected for review.
[2]Latest year's observation for March.
[3]Latest year's observation for June.
[4]Latest year's observation for September.
[5]Fiscal year.

economies. The same conclusion does not apply when dollarization reflects only asset substitution (the holding of foreign-currency-denominated assets as stores of value).

- Dollarization requires the adoption of special prudential measures. The banking system must be able to withstand significant exchange rate adjustments, as well as possibly larger-than-normal swings in capital flows. To deal with the latter, commercial banks or the central bank need to hold a larger-than-normal volume of international reserves, or to arrange external lines of credit. Limits to banks' foreign exposure positions need to be monitored carefully, as do off-balance-sheet operations that could entail foreign exchange risk. Since devaluations cannot shrink the value of dollar claims, steps have to be taken to ensure that banks do not incur undue risks in lending to dollar borrowers that do not have the capacity to honor their obligations when devaluations occur.

- Should dollarization be discouraged? The answer depends on the role of dollarization in the economy. Asset substitution may be a natural accompaniment of the opening of financial markets, and in this respect it should be welcome. Moreover, globalization of financial markets will likely lead to some dollarization.[4] Nonetheless, as with other forms of capital market liberalization, the proper sequencing of policies is essential. Asset substitution—and more especially, currency substitution—may also reflect the absence of macroeconomic stability and the existence of distortions in financial markets. In these circumstances, dollarization may complicate stabilization and cause additional volatility. However, in circumstances where it becomes very difficult to reestablish quickly stability of the national currency, economic well-being would likely be reduced by any administrative measures to reduce dollarization, and a case might be made for acceptance of continued dollarization in the quest for stability.

- Macroeconomic stability is the first priority in dealing with dollarization, but this may not, in and of itself, be sufficient to reverse it. Other measures, such as the liberalization of domestic interest rates, the establishment of a competitive domestic currency payments system, and the development of domestic financial instruments are also steps that can help "dedollarize" an economy. More direct measures to reverse dollarization, however, can be problematic. Regulatory limits on FCD or punitive reserve requirements on dollar deposits may simply drive dollars offshore, while forced conversions will undermine confidence and may also encourage capital flight.

[4]Other special circumstances may lead to dollarization. For instance, European countries that will not initially participate in the euro arrangements but that trade heavily with euro members are likely to see part of the demand for money shift to euros. In addition, very small economies in which tourism from abroad is an important sector are also likely to be dollarized.

• In general, IMF programs have treated dollarization as a symptom to be lived with rather than directly attacked and have concentrated on macroeconomic stabilization, in common with programs for nondollarized economies. In fact, dollarized countries with IMF programs have done only slightly worse in terms of meeting inflation targets than nondollarized economies with programs, although there is evidence of higher volatility in the former group. In some cases, concerns have arisen regarding the soundness of the banking system in dollarized economies. In other cases, the conventional practice of treating required reserves on FCD as a domestic, rather than foreign, liability may have put program objectives at risk. More broadly, program design in the presence of dollarization requires a more thorough analysis than usual in the selection of intermediate monetary targets and of the relationship of dollarization with ultimate targets.

II Trends and Explanations

In general terms, dollarization is a response to economic instability and high inflation, and to the desire of domestic residents to diversify their asset portfolios. In conditions of hyperinflation, dollarization is typically quite widespread because the public seeks protection from the cost of holding assets denominated in domestic currency. But, remarkably, the increase in dollarization in some Latin American and Asian countries has continued and even accelerated in recent years following successful stabilization. Some authors have pointed to ratchet effects in currency substitution to explain this development. But there is suggestive data indicating that the increase in local holdings of dollar assets in the 1990s also resulted from the reversal of capital flight and remonetization.

Currency Substitution Versus Asset Substitution

To understand these developments, it is useful to distinguish between two motives for the demand for foreign currency assets: currency substitution and asset substitution.[5] Currency substitution occurs when foreign-currency-denominated assets are used as a means of payment, while asset substitution occurs when foreign-currency-denominated assets serve as financial assets (store of value) but not as a means of payment or unit of account. Currency substitution typically arises under conditions of high inflation or hyperinflation when the high cost of using domestic currency for transactions prompts the public to look for alternatives. Asset substitution results from the public's allocation decisions in view of the risk and return characteristics of domestic and foreign assets. Historically, foreign-currency-denominated assets have provided the opportunity of insuring against major macroeconomic risks in many developing countries. Where indexed monetary assets have been available, as in Chile and Brazil, dollarization has been much less widespread, suggesting that indexation may be an alternative to dollarization in the face of macroeconomic instability. Even in countries that currently enjoy stability, foreign-currency-denominated assets may still provide insurance against the probability, small though it may be, of a return to inflation and devaluation, and they may also contribute to a reduction in overall risk in a balanced portfolio.[6]

Because of their close connection with monetary developments, this section focuses on three types of dollar-denominated financial assets: FCD in the domestic banking system, dollar currency in circulation within the domestic economy (DCC), and cross-border deposits held at banks abroad (CBD). The last of these may not be considered representative of dollarization because it is located abroad, but it is highly relevant because of its close substitutability with FCD. Because reliable information is available only for FCD, most studies are based on this measure only.[7] But even the incomplete information available on the other assets can shed some light on recent developments.[8]

Foreign Currency Deposits

FCD constitute a significant share of broad money in several developing countries and transition economies that have made use of IMF resources in recent years, reaching over 50 percent in Azerbaijan, Bolivia, Cambodia, Croatia, Nicaragua, Peru, and Uruguay in 1995 (see Table 1). An FCD ratio of

---

[5]This distinction is standard in the literature. See the useful surveys by Calvo and Végh (1996) and Giovannini and Turtelboom (1994). McKinnon (1996) terms the two motives direct currency substitution and indirect currency substitution.

[6]While the discussion in this paper focuses chiefly on the assets of the public, dollarization of deposits has typically been accompanied by dollarization of lending.

[7]Previous empirical studies on dollarization conducted in the IMF include those by Agénor and Khan (1996), Clements and Schwartz (1993), El-Erian (1988), Mueller (1994), Sahay and Végh (1996), Savastano (1992), and Savastano (1996).

[8]Dollarization as asset substitution is also associated with other nonmonetary assets, such as foreign-currency-denominated stocks and bonds and borrowing in foreign currency. But these assets are more removed from monetary developments and are considered more tangentially in this study.

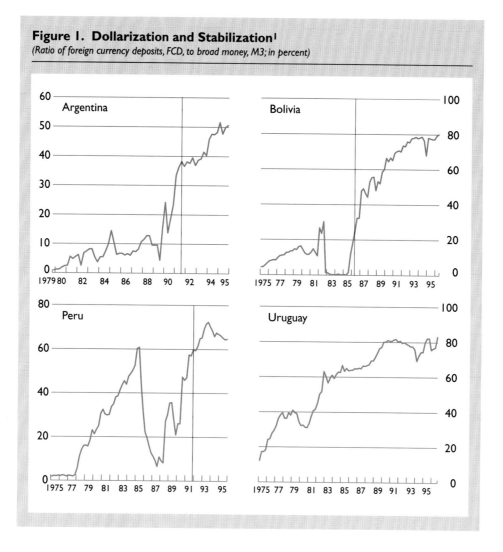

Figure I. Dollarization and Stabilization[1]
(Ratio of foreign currency deposits, FCD, to broad money, M3; in percent)

around 15–20 percent appears common in countries where residents are allowed to maintain foreign currency accounts. On account of their large size, persistence, and volatility over time, FCD developments in two regions—Latin America and the transition economies of Eastern Europe and the former Soviet Union—are particularly worth highlighting. Figure 1 displays the ratio of FCD to broad money (inclusive of FCD) for a selected group of countries in these two regions.[9]

With the advent of market reforms in the transition economies during the early 1990s, restrictions on FCD were generally eased (Sahay and Végh, 1996). As a result, the FCD ratio rose rapidly, reaching peak levels of 30–60 percent in most transition

economies during the 1990–95 period (see Table 1). High inflation rates, negative real interest rates on domestic-currency-denominated assets, and sharp devaluations that increased the domestic currency value of dollar deposits contributed to the rise in the FCD ratio. Following price stabilization, the FCD ratio declined sharply in countries such as Armenia, Estonia, Poland, and Mongolia. The valuation effect of substantial real appreciation also contributed to this decline, since it more than offset the rise in the dollar volume of FCD in several cases.

Abstracting from the periods when the convertibility of FCD was suspended, the ratio of FCD to broad money (inclusive of FCD) increased steadily in several Latin American countries during the 1970s and the 1980s, in a period of high inflation and a gradual easing of restrictions on FCD (Savastano, 1996). The 1990s witnessed a further easing of FCD restrictions in most countries, and FCD ratios continued to rise despite a sharp deceleration in in-

---

[9]In Africa, (measured) dollarization is less widespread than in other areas because FCD are not allowed or are severely restricted in most cases. However, there are indications of extensive dollarization in banknotes.

Figure 1 (*concluded*)

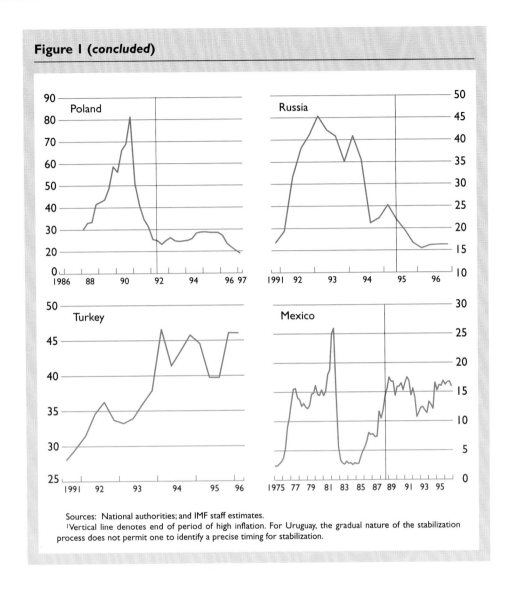

Sources: National authorities; and IMF staff estimates.
¹Vertical line denotes end of period of high inflation. For Uruguay, the gradual nature of the stabilization process does not permit one to identify a precise timing for stabilization.

flation rates, reaching 80 percent in Bolivia and Uruguay, over 60 percent in Peru, and nearly 50 percent in Argentina by 1995–96 (see Figure 1).

Although the history of high inflation and financial instability is closely linked to the prevalence of dollarization in several Latin American countries, it is remarkable that the FCD ratio *increased* sharply *after* countries successfully battled inflation in the late 1980s and early 1990s. (The approximate time of stabilization is shown by the vertical line in Figure 1.) One possible explanation is "hysteresis" or some form of nonreversibility in the process of dollarization (see Guidotti and Rodríguez, 1992). This could emerge, for example, because changing uses and practices regarding the settlement of transactions is a slow process that involves (informal) institutional changes and takes place only when there are significant benefits to be gained by switching currencies.

For the same reasons, a reversal of dollarization after stabilization would also be slow, especially if there are no significant benefits to be gained from switching back to the domestic currency as a means of payment.[10] It is also possible that financial innovation and liberalization have permanently reduced the cost of holding assets denominated in dollars.

Cross-Border Deposits

While the hysteresis argument may explain the persistence of dollarization, it would still not account for the cases of steady increase in dollarization after stabi-

---

[10]Kamin and Ericsson (1993) estimated a money demand function with "ratchet" effects for Argentina for a period that includes a hyperinflation episode.

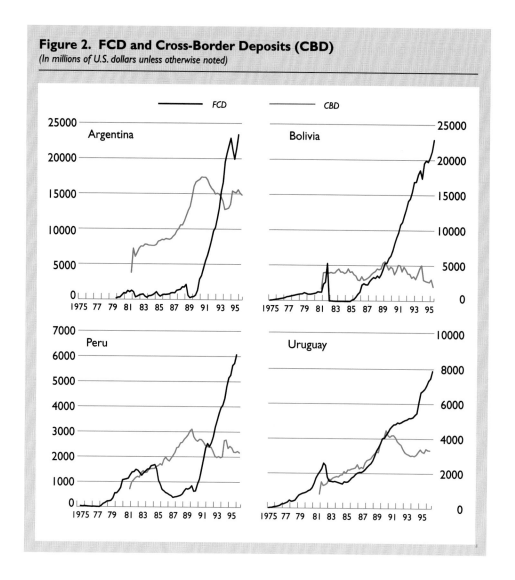

Figure 2. FCD and Cross-Border Deposits (CBD)
(In millions of U.S. dollars unless otherwise noted)

lization. The surge in capital inflows to developing countries in the 1990s offers an additional, or perhaps alternative, explanation for the persistent growth in the FCD ratio in the poststabilization period in Latin American countries.[11] It is quite suggestive that the increase in FCD (in dollar terms) coincided with the decrease in CBD in the 1990s for various Latin American countries, including the short-lived reversal in the cases of Mexico and Argentina at the time of the Mexican peso crisis (Figure 2). This suggests that the increase in FCD in part reflected a shift in residents' portfolios from CBD to dollar deposits in the domestic banking system. In this sense, the increase in domestic dollarization would reflect an increase in confidence in the domestic economy (although not necessarily in the domestic currency), rather than a persistent lack of

credibility.[12] This could be part of the process of general remonetization of the economy, as well as an increase in dollar-denominated lending by domestic banks. Moreover, because the persistent increase in the FCD ratio seems to be related to shifts from CBD to FCD, it is possible that the increase in the volume of FCD does not represent an increased volume of overall dollar assets. If a more comprehensive measure were available, one inclusive of cash and cross-

---

[11]Calvo and Végh (1992, 1996) and Savastano (1992, 1996) also mention capital flows as a driving factor for dollarization.

---

[12]While it is true that, according to available data, the decline in CBD is less than the increase in FCD in absolute terms, it should be noted that the CBD figures are likely to underestimate the actual stock of CBD. For legal and tax-related reasons, residents of one country may wish to transfer assets to a company based in a third country, which appears to be the holder of the deposit. (In fact, the three top countries of residence of nonbank depositors in the Western Hemisphere are Cayman Islands, Panama, and the Netherlands Antilles.) This means that the actual decline in CBD was probably larger than reported.

Figure 2 (concluded)

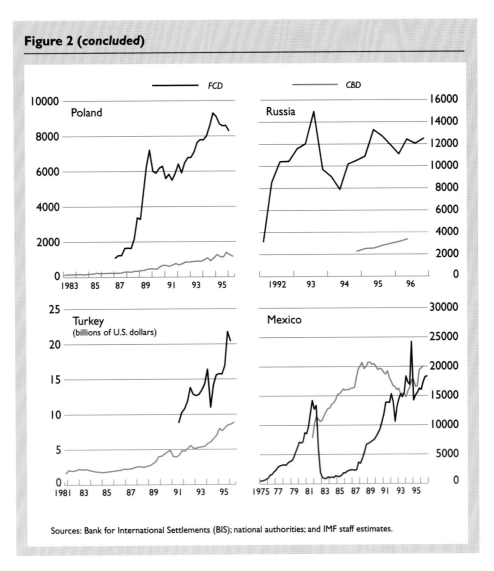

Sources: Bank for International Settlements (BIS); national authorities; and IMF staff estimates.

border deposits, the share of this broader set of foreign currency assets might even be seen to be declining.

Dollar Currency in Circulation

Although estimates of the amount of DCC in the home country do not exist, there is some suggestive data on flows of U.S. currency to other countries, collected from U.S. Customs forms called Currency and Monetary Instruments Reports (CMIR), which are completed when currency in amounts of $10,000 or higher is physically transported into or out of the United States.[13] The data displayed in Table 2 show

strikingly large flows of U.S. currency to several developing countries. The cumulation of net flows into these countries since 1989 reaches or exceeds 12 percent of GDP for Argentina (Box 1), Bolivia, Latvia, Russia, and Uruguay and exceeds DCC by a factor of two to three. One obvious shortcoming of these data is that much of the currency shipped to some countries ends up in third countries (or returns to the United States without being recorded) via capital outflows, tourism expenditures, and so on. In Russia, for example, "shuttle" trade (imports by individuals who cross borders to purchase goods in other countries) is conducted mainly in cash. In Argentina, significant outflows of dollar currency have also apparently taken place, including a large volume related to international tourism (Kamin and Ericsson, 1993).

The experience of Latin American and transition economies suggests several stylized facts. First, as restrictions are lifted, the FCD ratio can be expected

---

[13]These data have been kindly made available by the U.S. Treasury Department (Financial Crime Enforcement Network); this is the first time this information has been released with the exception of the data for Argentina used by Kamin and Ericsson (1993).

Table 2. Cumulative Net Inflows of U.S. Dollar Currency, 1989–96

Country	In Millions of U.S. Dollars	In U.S. Dollars per Capita	As Percent of Local Currency in Circulation	As Percent of GDP	As Percent of Foreign Currency Deposits
Argentina	34,737	1,014	294	12.4	147.8
Bolivia	831	103	290	11.9	36.2
Brazil	1,890	12	17	0.3	…
Estonia	43	28	12	1.2	…
Hungary	23	2	1	0.1	…
Latvia	822	316	173	18.4	…
Peru	636	27	51	1.1	10.4
Poland	609	16	7	0.5	7.3
Romania	44	2	3	0.1	…
Russia	43,772	294	246	12.2	382.4
Turkey	3,648	60	110	2.8	17.8
Ukraine	37	1	2	0.0	…
Uruguay	2,104	662	442	11.8	26.5
Venezuela	1,191	54	141	1.8	…

Sources: Data on cumulative net dollar currency flows from the United States from 1989 through 1996 from Financial Crimes Enforcement Network, U.S. Department of the Treasury, as recorded in the Customs Service Currency and Monetary Instruments Reports (CMIR) forms. See text for discussion. Other data from IMF, *IFS*, and from national authorities (central bank bulletins).

Box 1. Flows of U.S. Dollar Cash to Argentina

Despite shortcomings, the data from U.S. Customs Currency and Monetary Instruments Reports (CMIR) can be informative, as the depicted evolution of net dollar cash inflows to Argentina suggests. At times of financial insecurity there are sharp increases in the shipment of U.S. dollar currency into the country. This is noticeable in the two spikes in the first figure. The first spike took place at the time of the Mexican crisis (end-1994/early 1995), and the second one at the time of the resignation of Minister Cavallo in July 1996. The second figure shows that the increase in DCC (obtained from cumulative flows) parallels that of FCD, except for a movement in the opposite direction at the time of the Mexican crisis (1994–95), which presumably reflects a run on domestic dollar deposits. This evidence suggests that DCC may function partly as CBD (as suggested by the flight from FCD to CBD *and* DCC during the Mexican crisis) and partly as a complement to FCD (as suggested by the general growing trend in both aggregates). While this information does not permit one to construct firm estimates, it is suggestive of the magnitude and relevance of the stock of DCC in dollarized economies.

Argentina: Net Inflow of Dollar Cash per Quarter
(In billions of U.S. dollars)

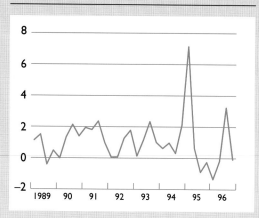

Argentina: Stocks of Foreign Currency Deposits, Dollar Cash, and Cross-Border Deposits per Quarter
(In billions of U.S. dollars)

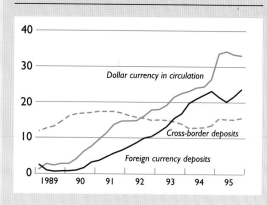

to increase as the public takes advantage of the opportunity to diversify its asset portfolio or to repatriate funds that were held in other countries. Where restrictions are suddenly removed, as in some transition economies, a distinct stock adjustment can be observed. Second, the existence of macroeconomic imbalances reflected in high inflation rates can lead to currency substitution, especially when other inflation-protected liquid financial assets are not available and more so in situations of hyperinflation. Third, currency substitution can persist even after countries have successfully brought down inflation rates, especially when they previously experienced long periods of inflation. Finally, even in the absence of currency substitution, dollarization in the form of asset substitution can be a permanent feature, especially as the process of financial deepening and globalization advances.

III   Risks and Benefits of Dollarization

In a fully liberalized and convertible financial system, savers would prefer to hold a portion of their portfolio in foreign-currency-denominated assets, simply in order to achieve a desired distribution of risk and returns. But such diversification may increase systemic risks when financial systems are still immature and subject to many distortions. Therefore, dollarization of financial systems in developing countries presents both advantages and risks. On the one hand, allowing FCD in the domestic financial system provides the opportunity to allow greater domestic intermediation. On the other hand, because of currency risk and potential balance of payments problems, the systemic risks are high, and dollarization could increase the potential for financial and banking crises. These considerations imply that the speed with which it would be advisable to advance toward a fully convertible financial system and the proper timing for the liberalization of FCD and loans will be determined by the conditions prevailing in specific cases.

Benefits

Allowing FCD in the domestic financial system enhances the opportunity for *reintermediation* in economies that have undergone periods of very high inflation and unstable macroeconomic conditions, during which agents may have become reluctant to hold deposits in the banking system. With a restoration of stability, it is likely that confidence will be rebuilt only gradually. The availability of FCD can speed up this process to the extent that agents may be more willing to return to domestic intermediaries if they can hold dollar-denominated assets.

Allowing FCD also promotes *financial deepening*. Domestic banks can expand their operations rapidly by competing for the FCD held by residents in cross-border accounts. In fact, the growth of domestic banks would be somewhat limited if they were not allowed to offer FCD, since residents are unlikely to reduce significantly the share of their savings held in the form of dollar financial assets for some time. In addition, the existence of dollar accounts in domestic

banks could facilitate the integration of the domestic market into the rest of the world and lower the cost of international financial transactions. Also, in case of fear of devaluation, the availability of FCD may encourage depositors to shift at least part of their local currency deposits (LCD) into FCD rather than CBD.[14]

Allowing residents to hold FCD can increase *credibility* by raising the cost of monetary indiscipline, thus committing the government to stronger financial policies. Similar arguments have been made to support the introduction of indexed government debt. A similar type of commitment strategy is to issue dollar-denominated debt to domestic residents as a substitute for domestic currency debt. However, it is not always the case that "raising the stakes" in this form will guarantee sound policies or avoid crises, and the costs of a crisis would be higher if one did occur.[15] Furthermore, when confidence is very weak, it would appear that a different type of monetary framework, such as a currency board, would be more effective, both to bolster financial discipline and to reinforce confidence. When even this is not sufficient to strengthen the government's financial discipline sufficiently, full dollarization—abolition of the domestic currency altogether—could indeed be the only alternative to achieve price stability. This would entail certain losses for the country: forgoing seignorage, limitations to the lender of last resort function, and the loss of the exchange rate instrument. It is true, however, that the value of these resources and instruments is limited in economies that are overwhelmingly dollarized.[16] Yet full dollarization, being difficult to re-

---

[14]For a discussion of this issue for the case of Argentina, see Garcia-Herrero (1997).

[15]The issuance by the Mexican government of the dollar-indexed tesobonos in 1994 signaled a commitment to a fixed exchange rate and raised the risks involved in a potential reversal of capital flows. On balance, it does not appear that tesobonos had a positive effect on credibility. As suggested by Drazen and Masson (1994), one has to distinguish between credibility of policy makers and credibility of policies, and the latter was very low in this case.

[16]The exchange rate instrument could still be effective to induce changes in relative prices if domestic prices are not rigid in dollar terms; that is, if the domestic currency is the predominant unit of account in the economy.

verse, effectively precludes the possibility of a recovery in the demand for domestic money.

Risks

On the negative side, a rapid development of dollar-denominated operations in the banking system increases the *risk of crisis* in financial and foreign exchange markets. Capital inflows intermediated by the banking system may expand gross official international reserves, with a parallel increase in domestic short-run liabilities in the form of the increase in banks' required reserves with the monetary authorities. Unless the monetary authorities hold all the resultant increase in required reserves in foreign exchange reserves, there will be a deterioration in their net foreign-currency-denominated position. Moreover, the rapid expansion in dollar deposits and loans that may result from a return of flight capital is likely to increase the riskiness of the loan portfolio of the domestic banks. Although this increase in risk would also develop in the domestic-currency loan portfolio, an important difference is that the expansion in loans and deposits under the fractional reserve banking system implies that the total volume of dollar-denominated assets and liabilities will greatly exceed the volume of *net* dollar assets held in the economy. This lessens the central bank's ability to act effectively as lender of last resort and increases the vulnerability of the banking system to capital outflows.[17] Maturity mismatches between bank assets and liabilities in foreign currency would increase banks' vulnerability to volatile capital flows. For example, withdrawal of short-term, dollar credits from banks forced the Mexican authorities to provide substantial dollar loans to the banking system in early 1995.[18] Further, in the case of a devaluation, loan defaults would increase, and the financial position of banks deteriorate, unless dollar lending is largely to debtors whose net financial position benefits from a devaluation, for example exporters. In fact, the central bank may attempt to avoid significant devaluations because of the likely negative effect on the quality of the banks' loan portfolios, even if there were otherwise valid macroeconomic reasons to devalue.

Dollarization also implies the loss of *seignorage* revenues for the monetary authorities (see Fischer, 1982). Other things equal, the use of foreign currency reduces the demand for domestic money and implies a lower level of seignorage for the government. While the central bank may earn some seignorage from below-market remuneration of banks' required reserves in foreign currency, it cannot avoid seignorage losses that result from foreign currency in circulation. The data on flows of U.S. dollar currency to various dollarized economies (see Table 2) suggest that the circulation of foreign currency, and thus the potential seignorage losses, is indeed substantial in some of the more dollarized economies. For example, if the ratio of U.S. dollar currency to GDP is 10 percent, and monetary aggregates grow at an average of 15 percent a year, seignorage losses would amount to 1.5 percent of GDP a year.[19]

---

[17]Moreover, unlike with loans in local currency, the burden of foreign currency loans (FCL) could not be reduced through devaluation.

[18]As noted earlier, the problems described in this paragraph would also apply to banking systems exposed to foreign exchange risk because they are heavily engaged in foreign exchange transactions. However, such exposure is likely to be more pervasive in countries in which there is extensive currency or asset substitution.

[19]The magnitude of the seignorage revenues obtained by the United States from the holding of its currency in foreign countries is relatively small. It is estimated that $200 to $250 billion circulated outside the United States in 1995 (Porter and Judson, 1996). If there was no such foreign demand for the U.S. currency, and the United States had to issue an equivalent amount of short-term treasury bills, the annual interest cost would be some $10 billion to $15 billion, less than ¼ of 1 percent of GDP.

IV Monetary and Exchange Rate Policy in a Dollarized Economy

The phenomenon of dollarization poses a challenge to the pursuit of a coherent and independent monetary policy. In responding to this challenge, the authorities must address two key questions about the conduct of monetary policy. What is the most appropriate exchange rate/monetary policy regime? What monetary target should the authorities pursue (in particular, should dollar-denominated assets be included in an intermediate target)? This section addresses these two questions in turn. To organize ideas, it is useful to discuss the cases of currency substitution and asset substitution separately, while bearing in mind that in practice the two may coexist. Currency substitution would in general be accompanied by asset substitution, since it is natural to hold financial assets denominated in the transaction currency. In contrast, asset substitution does not necessarily involve currency substitution.

Exchange Rate Regime

The theoretical literature suggests that a key implication of *currency substitution* is that the volatility of a floating exchange rate will tend to be greater. First, there may be frequent and unexpected shifts in the use of domestic and foreign money for transaction purposes. Because the two currencies serve essentially the same purpose, the public may shift between them for a number of not easily identifiable reasons.[20] Second, domestic money demand (the demand for the domestic component of the monetary aggregate) will be more sensitive to changes in its expected opportunity cost. In addition to the usual effect of interest rates on overall money demand, the domestic component of money will also be affected by changes in its opportunity cost relative to foreign money. In other words, the interest elasticity of domestic money demand will be higher when currency substitution is significant. While the implications of

this higher interest elasticity depend in a complex way on the structure of the economy, one important effect is that in a floating-rate system, the exchange rate will be more sensitive to expected changes in the domestic money supply and other variables that affect the money market. The higher elasticity may also have the opposite effect, however, for different types of shocks. For example, a given random shock to current money demand will have smaller overall effects, since smaller changes in the exchange rate and interest rates would be required to bring the money market back into equilibrium.

A clear case for fixing the exchange rate in a highly dollarized economy is when stabilizing from very high inflation or hyperinflation. Currency substitution is likely to be important, and monetary shocks are likely to predominate, especially because successful stabilization may result in a large but unpredictable increase in demand for domestic currency. Moreover, in a hyperinflation, foreign currency may assume the role of unit of account, and the exchange rate may also serve as an approximate measure of the price level, which would make the role of fixing the exchange rate very powerful in guiding expectations toward a low-inflation equilibrium. The stabilization from hyperinflation in Argentina in 1991 and in Croatia in 1994 are examples where an exchange rate anchor helped to stop inflation in its tracks within the context of extensive currency substitution.[21]

Dollarization in the sense of *asset substitution* alone does not directly affect a narrow definition of money demand. The availability of dollar deposits in domestic banks, however, has several implications for monetary policy. The most important for the choice of exchange rate regimes may be that the availability of dollar deposits in domestic banks also

---

[20]For example, in several transition economies, a decline in the acceptability of $100 bills (owing to fears that they would be confiscated during the conversion to the new notes) appears to have briefly raised the demand for domestic currency.

[21]This conclusion applies not only to exchange rate systems in which the rate is formally pegged but also to exchange-rate-based stabilizations more generally; that is, situations in which macroeconomic policies (monetary policy in particular) are geared to maintaining a stable exchange rate continuously, even though the exchange arrangement is flexible. In Croatia, the anchor was not an explicit, formal one, but ex post this episode can be considered as an instance of exchange-rate-based stabilization.

serves to increase capital mobility, since the public can potentially shift between dollar-denominated deposits held with domestic banks and abroad, and between dollar- and domestic-currency-denominated deposits held with domestic banks. These different assets are likely to be close substitutes from the point of view of savers, and this in turn strengthens the links between interest rates in dollar deposits at home, international dollar interest rates, and domestic currency interest rates. This would limit the control that the central bank can exert on monetary conditions, such as the level of interest rates on domestic currency. In this respect, a flexible exchange arrangement may be a useful device to increase monetary autonomy, which somewhat contradicts the general recommendation in the currency substitution case.

It is in principle possible to make a judgment about the extent to which dollarization represents currency substitution rather than asset substitution. Countries with a history of hyperinflation are prime candidates for currency substitution, even if they currently enjoy price stability. In general, when currency substitution is widespread there is anecdotal evidence of its existence. Large DCC would be an a priori indicator of currency substitution, as would a predominance of demand deposits among the dollar-denominated deposits or a well-developed dollar money market. However, in cases where dollar deposits are not legal, the banking system is not trusted or is underdeveloped (as in Indochina), or where the fear of confiscation is high, foreign currency may be demanded as a safe asset rather than for currency substitution reasons.

Choice of Monetary Target

In a floating exchange rate regime, or a fixed exchange rate regime with limited capital mobility, dollarization can affect the choice of intermediate targets of monetary policy. On the view that money is targeted because it determines the price level through transaction demand for money, currency substitution implies that dollar monetary assets are part of the relevant concept of money, whereas asset substitution implies that they are not.

The empirical literature has shed little light on the distinction between currency substitution and asset substitution in this context. Most work has implicitly or explicitly assumed away asset substitution in testing for currency substitution.[22] The traditional approach has been to attempt to identify currency substitution from the coefficients on the rate of return variables included in money demand functions.

Specifically, studies added a variable measuring expected exchange rate depreciation to the usual determinants of domestic money demand and interpreted this variable as measuring the opportunity cost of holding domestic versus foreign *currency*.[23] As Cuddington (1983) pointed out, however, domestic money demand will depend on the rate of exchange rate depreciation even in the absence of currency substitution, because the rate of depreciation affects the yield of foreign assets, which is an opportunity cost to domestic money. Thus, a test to distinguish between currency and asset substitution would include both the rate of return on foreign bonds in domestic currency and the rate of depreciation itself in the money demand regression, with a negative and significant coefficient on the rate of depreciation variable suggesting currency substitution as distinct from asset substitution. Unfortunately, these two rates of return variables are closely correlated, particularly in countries likely to have currency substitution, and their independent effects are essentially impossible to distinguish.

In this light, a potentially more fruitful approach to identifying currency substitution would start not with money demand but with the determinants of inflation. Although money demand functions look quite similar to asset demand functions, and the explanatory variables that may distinguish between the two are highly correlated, it is the stock of money, but presumably not of assets, that is closely correlated with the volume of transactions and the rate of inflation. From this point of view, the relevant test of currency substitution is whether foreign monetary assets belong in the monetary aggregate that predicts inflation in the most reliable way.

Reasoning along these lines, Berg, Borensztein, and Chen (1997) used a vector autoregression methodology to examine the strength of the relationship between inflation and lagged changes in various definitions of money in Peru.[24] They found evidence suggesting that aggregates that include FCD improve inflation prediction in this bivariate framework. Although broad, purely domestic currency aggregates performed worse than narrow domestic currency aggregates, broad aggregates that include FCD did better. Moreover, they found that an even broader aggregate, one that also includes CBD, is the best predictor of inflation. These results suggest that aggregates including dollar deposits might be appropriate targets in Peru. However, there is little

---

[22]See Savastano (1996) for a useful review of this literature.

[23]See, for example, Miles (1978) and Bordo and Choudri (1982).

[24]A number of studies, including Estrella and Mishkin (1996), Friedman and Kuttner (1996), and Feldstein and Stock (1994), have used this type of technique to approach the analogous question of which monetary aggregate is the most appropriate focus of targeting.

reason to expect that this conclusion, illustrative as it is even for Peru, will be the same in each economy or that it will be the same over time, implying a need for country-specific investigation.[25]

The choice of a target monetary aggregate in dollarized economies is, therefore, essentially an empirical matter because it is not possible to deduce a priori the asset composition of money demand. Thus, the design of a monetary program would require an empirical investigation of the question whether the monetary aggregate that is most closely associated with the final objective—say the inflation rate—includes foreign-currency-denominated assets. Targeting the "wrong" aggregate—for example, one that excludes FCD when in fact the more stable relationship is with one that includes it—would be similar to targeting any monetary aggregate that has a loose or unstable relationship to final targets. The intermediate target variable will carry information, and targeting it will be less effective. Frequent revisions to intermediate target values would become

necessary, reducing the usefulness of the monetary targeting strategy.

The choice of a monetary aggregate as intermediate target for policy should be viewed, however, from the broader perspective of finding an aggregate that provides useful summary information on monetary conditions, rather than a target to be strictly pursued independent of the behavior of interest rates, the exchange rate, or other indicators.[26] While the question of the usefulness of money targeting is beyond the scope of this paper, it is worth remembering that the problem of selecting the appropriate monetary target is by no means exclusive to dollarized economies. It has proven difficult even in comparatively stable industrial countries to rely on targets for monetary aggregates in the conduct of monetary policy, and since the 1980s monetary targeting has become less and less common even in these countries. In this context, it is still to be expected that dollar deposits would play some role within the set of indicators that the central bank would need to watch in assessing monetary conditions.

---

[25]The finding for Peru may be affected by institutional changes that took place during the sample period. The Central Bank of Peru has found a narrow, purely domestic currency aggregate to be the most useful intermediate target.

[26]It may also be difficult to implement an intermediate target that includes foreign assets. The lack of reliable data on DCC would make it difficult to do so.

V   Operational Issues in Dollarized Economies

This section first reviews how monetary policy implementation and payments system arrangements have been adjusted in light of heavy dollarization and then discusses the implications of dollarization for prudential regulation and effective bank supervision, and the central bank's role of lender of last resort.

Implementation of Monetary Policy

Monetary operations can be conducted in either domestic or foreign currency instruments. Although conducting all monetary operations in local currency is simpler in principle and may be used to signal the central bank's support for its own currency, the currency of denomination of monetary instruments should be consistent with the main money markets in the economy, as well as with the authorities' monetary targets. Thus, at high levels of dollarization, where the local currency money market is thin, as in Bolivia, using dollar instruments is likely to be less costly and more effective in implementing monetary policy.[27] In practice, however, there is considerable variation in the choice of single or multicurrency monetary operations in dollarized economies: the transition countries and Peru, for example, use a single currency (their own), whereas other countries, such as Argentina, Bolivia, and Uruguay, use both local and foreign currency. Further, the degree of substitutability between dollar-denominated government bonds and dollar assets available outside the home country affects the effectiveness of foreign exchange monetary intervention. The higher is the degree of substitutability, the lower is the effectiveness of this instrument.[28]

The design of reserve requirements in a dollarized economy is a complex issue. The authorities need to set several interlinked parameters: the level, the remuneration, and the currency of denomination. How these are set affects the cost for banks in funding themselves in domestic vis-à-vis foreign currency and also has prudential implications; insofar as dollarization reflects currency substitution, the level of the requirement will also have monetary implications. The weights to be given to these considerations will differ in different situations, and this will affect the policy advice to be given.[29]

In heavily dollarized economies, foreign currency reserve requirements on FCD can play a useful role as automatic liquidity stabilizers (as in Bolivia, Peru, and Uruguay). When denominated in foreign currency, averaging reserve requirements over the holding period allows banks to draw flexibly on their reserves, limiting the need for central bank intervention in the dollar money market.[30] Reserve requirements on FCD can also be used to automatically sterilize or (when unremunerated) discourage capital inflows. However, as discussed below, heavy taxation of deposits puts a financial burden on banks and risks financial disintermediation. Moreover, frequent changes in reserve requirements are inadvisable because they complicate banks' liquidity management.

Implications for the Payments System

A question also arises whether commercial banks should be allowed to effect interbank settlement in dollars on the books of the central bank, as in Bolivia, Lebanon, Nicaragua, Peru, and Uruguay, or whether that should be done on the books of a commercial bank (domiciled locally or overseas; see Table 3).

---

[27]For similar reasons (a high degree of indexation), the Central Bank of Chile's main monetary instrument is an indexed instrument.

[28]For example, preliminary evidence suggests that the short-run offset coefficient for Uruguay is higher than that for Bolivia, which implies that foreign exchange monetary intervention would be a more effective instrument in Bolivia than in Uruguay. Offset coefficients measure the extent to which changes in the net foreign assets of the central bank resulting from open market operations are offset by market-originated opposite changes in those assets.

[29]For a discussion of these issues see Monetary and Exchange Affairs Department (1995).

[30]Thus, in Peru, central bank intervention in the dollar money market is unnecessary, owing to the very high reserve requirements on FCD, and wide limits on banks' open foreign exchange positions that facilitate arbitrage between the domestic currency and foreign currency financial markets.

Table 3. Payment and Regulatory Arrangements in Selected Dollarized Economies

Country	Currency Used	Clearing and Settlement in Foreign Currency	Domestic FCD	Domestic Foreign Currency Loans (FCL)	Cross-Border Deposits (CBD)
			Developing countries		
Argentina	Argentinean peso. Legal contracts can be denominated and settled in U.S. dollars.	Domestic wholesale transactions with dollar-denominated checking accounts can be cleared either through commercial bank accounts in the central bank or using New York banks through Clearing House Integrated Payment System orders and settled through correspondent accounts of banks located in New York.	Restriction on holdings of FCD were eased in late 1978. Foreign currency savings and time deposits must be denominated in convertible currencies. The use of checking accounts denominated in U.S. dollars is allowed for domestic transactions.	No restrictions.	No restrictions.
Bolivia	Boliviano. Legal contracts can be denominated and settled in U.S. dollars.	Dollar checks are cleared privately and settled through foreign currency accounts in the Central Bank of Bolivia.	Restrictions on FCD were eased in October 1973. From end-1982 to mid-1985, U.S. dollar deposits were not allowed. In 1987, foreign currency checking deposits were permitted.	No restrictions.	No restrictions.
Egypt	Egyptian pound.	Private banks operate an informal interbank foreign currency clearing system.	No restrictions.	No restrictions.	Residents are allowed to hold accounts abroad.
Lebanon	Lebanese pound.	In 1990, the Bank of Lebanon established a clearing system for dollar-denominated checks. Before 1990, check clearing had only been offered by two private institutions.	Even before the civil war, residents were allowed to hold FCD in the domestic banking system. Dollarization increased after the war when economic conditions deteriorated.	No restrictions. However, banks may only on-lend up to 65 percent of FCD	No restrictions.

Country					
Peru	Nuevo sol. Legal contracts can be denominated and settled in U.S. dollars.	Clearing in U.S. dollars takes place manually at the clearing houses managed by the Central Reserve Bank of Peru with settlement using foreign currency accounts of commercial banks at the CRBP. In addition, a private electronic clearing arrangement is operated by a group of ten banks with final settlement using foreign currency central bank accounts. The latter system accounts for a small volume of total transactions.	Restrictions on the holdings of FCD were eased in early 1978. FCD were declared inconvertible in July 1985 and banned in July 1987. While demand and time deposits were allowed once more in September 1988, savings deposits were allowed in August 1990. However, FCD only regained full convertibility in August 1990.	Currently, no restrictions. However, from 1979 to 1990 (with the exception of the period in which FCD were banned), FCD were subject to marginal reserve requirements that were never below 90 percent.	No restrictions.
Philippines	Philippine peso. Various denominations of gold coins are also legal tender. Since the repeal of the Uniform Currency Act of 1996, legal contracts can be denominated in any currency.	Dollar-based interbank payments called Philippines Electronic Dollar Transfer System (PEDS) are done through the clearing system operated, at the moment, by Citibank. The maximum daylight overdraft that Citibank allows each bank is US$1 million. Settlement takes place at the end of the day, and if any counterpart fails to deliver on their gross dues, then their due-froms are also withheld, with no payments made.	Banks obtained large amounts of foreign exchange from FCD units after the foreign exchange system was deregulated in 1992.	Commercial banks may grant (1) private sector loans if serviced using foreign exchange to be sourced outside the banking system; (2) short-term loans to financial institutions for normal interbank transactions; and (3) short-term loans to commodity and service exporters and to importers. In practice, this regulation does not restrict FCL.	No restrictions.
Uruguay	Uruguayan peso. Legal contracts can be denominated and settled in U.S. dollars.	Clearing in U.S. dollars takes place manually at the clearing houses managed by the Central Bank of Uruguay with settlement using foreign currency accounts of commercial banks at the Central Bank of Uruguay (Information from 1993).	Restrictions on holdings of FCD were eased in October 1974. Since the 1980s, the Uruguayan financial system operates as an offshore center.	No restrictions.	No restrictions. (Commercial banks are not allowed to borrow abroad.)

Table 3 (concluded)

Economies in transition

Country	Currency Used	Clearing and Settlement in Foreign Currency	Domestic FCD	Domestic Foreign Currency Loans (FCL)	Cross-Border Deposits (CBD)
Poland	Zloty.	No domestic clearing in foreign currency.	Enterprises may maintain foreign currency accounts for external settlements. Since December 1995 foreign exchange proceeds from exports can be deposited in those accounts. Households may maintain FCD but may not use them to effect settlements between individuals or for business activity. Accounts in domestic currency are effectively convertible into foreign currency by withdrawing zlotys, converting them to dollars, and redepositing them.	No restrictions.	Resident households and enterprises who demonstrate proof of need may hold foreign exchange accounts abroad with the National Bank of Poland's permission. Balances in these accounts may not exceed US$100,000.
Vietnam	Vietnamese dong.	FCD in the domestic banking system may not be used for purely domestic payments.	Since 1988, households and enterprises are allowed to hold FCD in domestic commercial banks that are licensed to conduct foreign exchange business in Vietnam. Organizations and enterprises must deposit all foreign exchange proceeds in these accounts. Limits on foreign exchange holdings in such accounts are set by the commercial banks applying rules set by the central bank. Deposits in excess of those limits must be sold to commercial banks.	Domestic lending in foreign currency may be done only for trade-related financing.	Firms in the aviation, shipping, postal, and insurance sectors, as well as commercial banks, finance companies, and other firms permitted to open branches abroad may be granted permission to deposit foreign currency receipts from invisible transactions in foreign accounts.

Sources: IMF, Exchange Arrangements and Exchange Restrictions Database; and IMF staff.

Neither the central bank nor the commercial banks can create dollar reserves. Moreover, as illustrated by the experience of Bolivia, the choice of settlement bank may not have much impact on the pace of dollarization (Figure 3).[31] However, private settlement arrangements may be subject to systemic risk, since in a crisis the clearing bank may be unwilling to extend emergency support, may withdraw its normal settlement credit lines, or may fail.[32] Moreover, failure to settle dollar payments could trigger systemic failures that would affect both the domestic currency and dollar markets. In addition, the central bank loses seignorage if settlement balances are held with another bank. In heavily dollarized economies, those considerations argue in favor of settling interbank dollar balances on the books of the central bank, and in enabling the central bank to provide lender of last resort services in foreign currency, for which it would need an appropriate cushion of foreign reserves. Finally, the authorities should endeavor to ensure that payments services in domestic currency are able to compete in reliability and efficiency with those in foreign currency, so as not to provide an additional incentive for dollarization.[33]

Prudential Supervision

The strategic risks that dollarization can impart to banks' balance sheets were discussed in Section III. These risks relate primarily to the possibility of large capital outflows and exchange rate movements. The management of such risks is the broad responsibility of macroeconomic policy. In addition, however, prudential supervision and regulation need to take into account the risks of dollarization. The need to enhance banks' capacity to sustain loan losses after a devaluation adds another argument for banks in developing countries to exceed the Basle guidelines for capital adequacy.[34] Limits on foreign

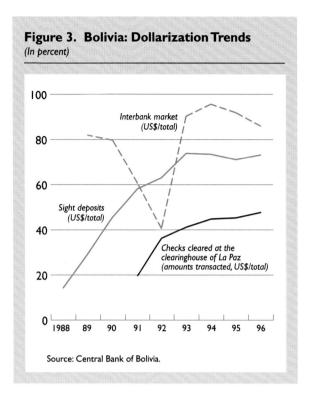

Figure 3. Bolivia: Dollarization Trends
(In percent)

Source: Central Bank of Bolivia.

exchange positions—following international standards—should be strictly enforced to contain foreign exchange risk.[35]

As noted earlier, reserve requirements on FCD, if matched by foreign currency reserves, can limit systemic liquidity risk. Since that risk is likely to be higher for FCD than for LCD, from a prudential point of view a case can be made for the former to bear a higher reserve requirement than the latter, as is the case in Bolivia, Honduras, Nicaragua, and Peru (Table 4).[36] Thus, the ratio of gross foreign assets of the central bank to M3 is substantially higher in Peru than in Bolivia, largely owing to Peru's much higher reserve requirements on FCD. Liquidity requirements can also perform the role of limit-

---

[31]The use of dollar sight deposits expanded rapidly in Bolivia after these accounts were authorized in 1988, notwithstanding that interbank clearing and settlement of checks drawn on these accounts was, until 1991, effected on the basis of private arrangements outside the central bank (see Figure 3).

[32]There is some evidence that Argentine branches of foreign banks cut their exposure in the interbank market in the aftermath of the Mexican crisis.

[33]This issue is illustrated by the case of the Philippines, where payments dollarization has been encouraged by the fact that the foreign currency payments system—where dollar transactions are sent on an electronic payments system operated by Citibank in Manila—technically dominates the peso payments system—which depends on the physical delivery of checks.

[34]For example, although primarily motivated by the restrictions imposed by the currency board arrangement rather than by dollarization, the capital adequacy ratio was raised to 11.5 percent in Argentina. Moreover, since Argentina applies more stringent criteria for weighting risky assets, that ratio is equivalent to about 16 percent under the Basle guidelines. In Bolivia, it will gradually be raised to 10 percent, reflecting concerns about dollarization as well as broader concerns about the soundness of the banking system. These compare with a Basle guideline of 8 percent.

[35]These requirements need not exceed those used for nondollarized economies, since foreign exchange exposure depends on a bank's net, rather than gross, position. Moreover, the risk on the bank's gross foreign currency position accrues from credit risk, rather than foreign exchange risk. However, to avoid circumvention via derivatives, foreign exchange open positions may need to be assessed on the basis of risk accounting principles (see Garber, 1996).

[36]However, other considerations—e.g., risk of capital flight—limit the scope for unremunerated reserve requirements on FCD.

Table 4. Reserve Requirements on FCD for Selected Countries[1]

(In percent; end-December 1996 unless otherwise noted)

Country	Reserve Requirements on Local Currency Deposits (LCD)	Reserve Requirements on FCD	Currency of Denomination of Reserve Requirements on FCD[2]	Ratio of FCD to Total Deposits
Developing countries				
Argentina[3]	17.0	17.0	F	50.0
Bolivia	10.0	20.0	F	92.0
Egypt	15.0	10.0	F	27.2
Guinea-Bissau	25.0	25.0	F	57.0
Honduras	12.0	50.0[4]	F	26.7
India	10.0	0.0	—	...
Jordan	14.0	14.0	F	18.5
Lebanon	13.0	0.0	—	53.7
Malawi	20.0	20.0	F	11.2
Malaysia	13.5	13.5	L	...
Maldives	35.0	35.0	F	50.3
Nepal	12.0	12.0	L	7.1
Nicaragua	15.0	25.0	F	64.4
Pakistan	5.0	5.0	L	...
Peru	9.0	45.0	F	74.7
Phillippines	17.0	0.0	—	48.4
São Tomé and Príncipe	15.0	30.0	F	45.6
Tanzania	12.0	0.0	—	25.0
Turkey	8.0	11.0	F	49.3
Economies in transition				
Albania	10.0	10.0	F	32.0
Armenia	12.0	12.0	LF	58.0
Belarus	15.0	15.0	L	31.3
Bulgaria	10.0	10.0	L	55.8
Cambodia	5.0	5.0	LF	92.7
Croatia[5]	35.9	60.0	F	68.0
Czech Republic	11.5	11.5	L	7.0
Estonia	10.0	10.0	L	15.5
Lao P.D.R.	12.0	12.0	L	49.0
Latvia	8.0	8.0	L	52.9
Lithuania	7.0	7.0	F	37.6
Poland	17.0	2.0	L	17.3
Romania	7.5	10.0	LF	23.4
Russia[6]	10.0	5.0	L	36.5
Slovak Republic	9.0	9.0	L	11.2
Uzbekistan	25.0	0.0	—	34.7
Vietnam	10.0	10.0	F	29.8
OECD countries				
Germany	2.0	2.0	L	0.6
Italy[7]	15.0	15.0	L	2.0
Japan	1.3	0.3	L	5.1
United Kingdom	0.4	0.4	L	15.7

Source: IMF, Monetary and Exchange Affairs Department, Information System on Monetary Instruments.

[1]Unless otherwise specified, ratio on demand deposits.

[2]L is local currency; F is foreign currency; LF commercial banks can deposit and hold reserves in local or foreign currency.

[3]Liquidity requirements; reserves on both LCD and FCD may be held abroad.

[4]Of which 12 percentage points must be held in vault cash and deposits in the central bank.

[5]Weighted average ratio on LCD; reserves on FCD are held abroad.

[6]As of end-March 1997; ratio on term deposits of more than 90 days.

[7]Applied on new deposits since June 1994.

ing systemic risk—at a lower cost to the banks—as has been done in Argentina.[37]

Some highly dollarized countries have imposed restrictions on FCL (foreign currency loans) to limit credit risks. In Lebanon, FCL are limited to 60 percent of FCD, forcing banks to hold the remainder in foreign currency assets abroad. In Vietnam, FCL may be given only for trade-related purposes. In Malaysia and the Philippines, dollar loans to the private sector can be made only to borrowers that generate an income in foreign currency. However, when FCD are high relative to LCD, strict restrictions on FCL may entail a severe limitation on the availability of credit for a given volume of total deposits.

Implications for the Central Bank

As lender of last resort, the central bank should ideally have foreign exchange reserves in sufficient quantity to forestall a run on FCD. The central bank (or the treasury) may also need reserves to support the market for dollar-denominated public securities.[38] The central bank's ability to secure its role as lender of last resort, or to ensure orderly conditions in the market for (dollar-denominated) public sector debt, can be enhanced by access to emergency credit lines from other central banks or from commercial banks.[39] In addition, allowing sound foreign banks, which can receive head office support in an emergency, to operate can also limit the need for central bank systemic support.

Supervisory authorities need to be particularly vigilant to ensure that financial institutions have the financial skills and the risk management arrangements to manage effectively the risks inherent in operating in a dual currency system. In particular, foreign currency exposures need to be monitored closely. These considerations apply also to banking systems that operate heavily in foreign currencies even if the economies in which they function are not dollarized. However, the problem is likely to be more widespread in dollarized economies, where banks are less likely to have a choice as regards the currency denomination of their operations.

Since a run on foreign currency bank deposits can destabilize a banking system (including the local currency segment), there is a case for including FCD in a country's deposit insurance arrangements. Care should be taken, however, to price that insurance properly, in order to avoid cross-subsidization.

---

[37]When liquidity requirements are fulfilled with domestic assets—rather than foreign liquid assets—the central bank needs to have sufficient foreign reserves to maintain the liquidity of these assets in the case of a systemic crisis. Liquidity requirements can take the form of fixed coefficients that can be differentiated by maturity of deposits to reflect differences in volatility (as in Argentina) or of limits on maturity mismatches. While more difficult to monitor, the latter also limit interest rate risk. As countries strengthen their supervisory capacity and banks improve their internal risk controls, liquidity requirements need to be substituted by more flexible and comprehensive methods to assess risk. See Gulde, Nascimento, and Zamalloa (1997).

[38]Mexico's experience with tesobonos in 1994 suggests that government bonds denominated in foreign currency *may be* sub-

ject to speculative attacks, particularly when they have short maturities and inadequate foreign reserve backing.

[39]Thus, in the wake of the Mexican crisis in 1994, a number of Asian central banks established a protocol for mutual liquidity support. Argentina established an arrangement that facilitates emergency borrowing from foreign commercial banks by local commercial banks. Although these examples are not specific to dollarized economies, similar arrangements can be tailored to them. See Baliño and others (1997).

VI   Measures to Affect Dollarization

The prerequisite to containing dollarization in an economy is always a sound macroeconomic policy. Also, institutional arrangements that bolster confidence in the maintenance of price stability—such as an independent central bank with a clear price stability mandate—can enhance confidence in the domestic currency and thereby reduce the degree of dollarization. As is argued above, however, it is possible for an economy to remain dollarized even after stabilization. This section discusses the various alternative measures available to limit dollarization and considers their effectiveness and drawbacks. It concludes that the most effective "dedollarization" measures are likely to be those that limit the *need* for dollar instruments. The least effective are those that directly restrict dollarization.

Alternative Financial Instruments

To limit dollarization, authorities may promote alternative financial instruments, such as stocks, mutual fund shares, corporate finance bonds, and asset-backed securities and also facilitate the use of specific indexed instruments or simple derivatives (swaps, futures, and options). These instruments, which are likely to be used mostly by enterprises and large investors, unbundle risk coverage from the transaction and store-of-value functions of currency. By limiting the replacement of local currency by foreign currency, including reserve money, those instruments in principle can enhance the scope for monetary policy. However, they are likely to be only partial substitutes for FCD and FCL—owing, for instance, to high transaction costs—and may be difficult to develop in unsophisticated markets. Furthermore, derivatives entail risks, to which the authorities should ensure that banks are not unduly exposed.

In several countries, dollar-indexed financial instruments provide an alternative to FCD. For example, in Bolivia and Nicaragua, dollar-indexed deposits coexist with dollar deposits.[40] The supply of

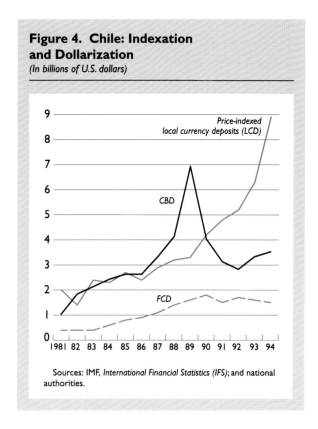

Figure 4. Chile: Indexation and Dollarization
(In billions of U.S. dollars)

Sources: IMF, *International Financial Statistics (IFS)*; and national authorities.

the former may be easier to influence because they are settled in domestic currency, which is under the control of the central bank. However, because of the uncertainty associated with the exchange rate at which dollar-indexed instruments can be effectively converted into dollars, particularly under systemic crisis conditions, these instruments are imperfect substitutes for FCD.[41]

Indexation with alternative indices, such as the price level or a short-term interest rate, can also reduce the risk associated with real returns on domestic currency deposits. In Brazil, while FCD have been

---

[40]The "mexdollar" system, which was widely used in Mexico until the forced conversion of deposits in August 1982, and the "Patzam" in Israel provide other illustrations.

[41]Thus, in Bolivia, their demand is mostly limited to public enterprises, which are required by law to hold their deposits in local currency. Similarly, in Nicaragua, dollar-indexed deposits pay a premium over dollar deposits.

strictly restricted, the relatively moderate capital flight suggests that indexation adequately met the public's demand for inflation protection.[42] In Chile, as has happened in some highly dollarized economies, price indexation is still widely used, despite the country's success in bringing inflation under control.[43] Although FCD are also available, they are small (Figure 4), which suggests that price indexation can be an effective substitute for dollarization. However, in considering indexation as an alternative to dollarization, the authorities need to evaluate carefully the benefits and risks. The latter include the danger of indexation being extended to the labor market and the difficulties this might create, including for bringing inflation down.

Policies That Create an Interest Rate Wedge

To the extent that portfolio choices are sensitive to relative prices, the dollarization of deposits can, in principle, be reduced through policies that create a wedge in favor of local currency interest rates. However, when those policies take the form of a tax on foreign currency intermediation, they run the risk of driving deposits overseas and reducing domestic lending.[44] Interest rate wedges will be the more effective in reversing dollarization to the extent that FCD are closer substitutes for LCD than for CBD, which can be the case in economies where confidence in the domestic economy has been restored.

Financial liberalization can permanently change the level of interest rates. Reflecting this, Egypt experienced a dramatic and lasting reversal in dollarization after liberalizing interest rates in 1991.[45] FCD decreased as a percentage of total deposits from over 60 percent in 1991 to less than 30 percent in 1996 (Figure 5).

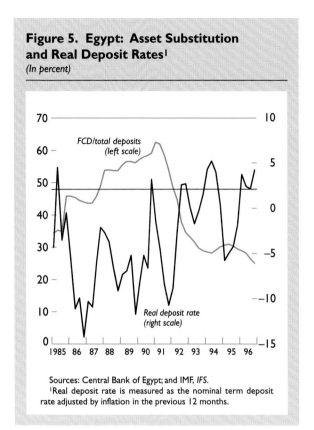

Figure 5. Egypt: Asset Substitution and Real Deposit Rates[1]
(In percent)

Sources: Central Bank of Egypt; and IMF, *IFS*.
[1]Real deposit rate is measured as the nominal term deposit rate adjusted by inflation in the previous 12 months.

Monetary policy may also induce interest rate wedges, although these are likely to be temporary.[46] Thus, in Hungary, the sharp increase in the interest rate spread during 1995–96 became ultimately unsustainable because it was associated with large capital inflows that could not be fully sterilized, and the wedge had only a small and transitory impact on dollarization (Figure 6).

Modifying the currency composition of domestic public debt or introducing differential reserve requirements can introduce a permanent wedge. Increasing the share of local currency domestic public debt at the expense of foreign currency domestic debt can increase interest rates in local currency and lower those in foreign currency. However, the higher interest rate on local currency loans reduces at the same time the demand for such loans and increases the share of FCL. In addition, the interest costs associated with such operations can quickly escalate.

Setting differential remuneration rates on reserve requirements on FCD introduces a wedge in banks' intermediation spreads, thereby in principle affecting dollarization measured both in terms of deposits

---

[42]In Brazil, both price indexation and interest rate indexation were broadly used. In particular, the indexation of deposits to the overnight interest rate protected the purchasing power of LCD throughout the turbulent inflationary period of the 1980s. However, the need to limit risks incurred by financial intermediaries in the overnight market eventually undermined the monetary anchor, since it induced pervasive monetary accommodation and led to the de facto creation of indexed money. See Garcia (1996).

[43]Price indexation has been facilitated by the introduction in 1967 of a unit of account, the UF, that is published by the central bank daily on the basis of the consumer price index.

[44]Also, since "dedollarization" measures are very difficult to apply to cash, part of the flow out of FCD can move to DCC.

[45]Other countries where financial liberalization may have contributed to limit dollarization include Armenia, Estonia, Lithuania, and Poland (see Sahay and Végh, 1996).

---

[46]A too tight monetary stance, if sustained, can have other adverse macroeconomic and financial implications, including an increase in the burden of public domestic debt.

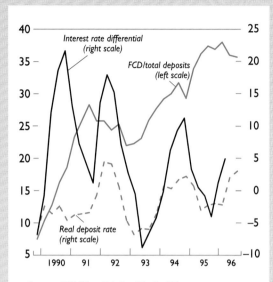

Figure 6. Hungary: Interest Rate Differential and Asset Substitution[1]

(In percent)

Sources: IMF, *IFS*; and National Bank of Hungary.

[1]Interest rate differential measured as domestic currency deposit rates as a percentage of Hungarian deposit rates adjusted for the previous 12-month depreciation rate. The use of the forward 12-month depreciation rate to calculate the interest differential does not yield a higher correlation coefficient (in absolute terms) between the interest rate differential and the ratio of FCD to total deposits.

and loans.[47] Thus, using such a technique Israel succeeded in the late 1980s in encouraging the substitution of dollar-indexed deposits ("Patzam") for dollar deposits ("Patam"). However, the effectiveness of reserve requirements in Israel was enhanced by the close substitutability of the Patam and Patzam. Other efforts to lower dollarization through high remunerated reserve requirements on FCD have been mostly inconclusive. In Nicaragua, the share of FCD in total deposits has increased during the period in which such requirements have been in effect. Inversely, in an effort to stimulate dollarization, El Salvador sharply reduced reserve requirements on FCD in April 1995. This led to only a small increase in asset substitution, suggesting that changes in reserve requirements—even when accompanied by clear policy announcements—can have only a limited impact

on dollarization when dollar assets are not close substitutes for local currency assets.[48]

Moreover, the scope for using reserve requirements to tax FCD is limited when such deposits can be substituted through off-balance-sheet transactions, informal intermediation, or derivatives. For instance, in Peru, where FCD are subject to a high reserve requirement (45 percent), banks have partially substituted offshore intermediation for domestic foreign currency intermediation.[49] In addition, banks circumvented reserve requirements on FCD through the use of domestic currency operations linked to the future foreign exchange rate. However, the central bank curtailed these operations when in 1995 it imposed on them the same requirement as on FCD.[50]

Direct Restrictions on Foreign Currency Deposits

The liberalization of regulations on FCD has often been followed by a rapid expansion of asset substitution. However, in countries where FCD had been allowed, measures to reverse that authorization through forced conversions, as in Bolivia and Mexico in 1982 and in Peru in 1985, had severe adverse effects. While FCD were initially substituted by LCD, the gain was only temporary (Figure 7), and FCD were later reintroduced. Moreover, the forced conversions entailed a substantial loss of government credibility and increased the confiscation risk perceived by domestic residents.[51]

Access to FCD can be limited, rather than prohibited. For example, in Mexico, only firms can hold FCD, and such holdings are limited as a proportion

---

[47]If the demand for dollar credits is elastic, an increase in unremunerated reserve requirements on FCD should have similar effects. When the demand for dollar credit is inelastic, an increase in unremunerated reserve requirements on FCD would raise dollar deposit rates and induce a capital inflow. Thus, dollarization, measured in terms of deposits, could rise.

[48]Reserve requirements were reduced from a uniform ratio of 50 percent to 30 percent and 20 percent, on demand and term deposits, respectively. While the share of FCL in total loans increased from 2.2 percent at end-1993 to 11 percent at end-April 1996, the share of FCD in total deposits increased from 3.8 percent at end-1993 to only 5.3 percent at end-April 1996.

[49]High reserve requirements on FCD were intended to limit short-term capital inflows and the associated prudential risk of rapid credit growth. In principle, this should also have encouraged the demand for LCD, but so far, probably owing to the low interest elasticity of LCD, growth in FCD has significantly outpaced growth in LCD. Between 1990 and 1996, end-of-year FCD balances increased from the equivalent of almost 3 percent of GDP to close to 14 percent of GDP, while LCD only grew from almost 2 percent of GDP to less than 5 percent over the same period.

[50]In Uruguay, which is an important regional offshore center, the authorities have also expressed the view that attempts to lower dollarization through high reserve requirements and similar measures would drive dollar deposits offshore.

[51]After FCD were later authorized again, Bolivian banks were subject to several incipient runs. The spread over LIBOR (London interbank offered rate) of dollar deposit rates, which reached over 900 basis points in 1987, was still over 400 basis points in December 1996.

Figure 7. Bolivia, Mexico, and Peru: Share of Deposits
(In percent)

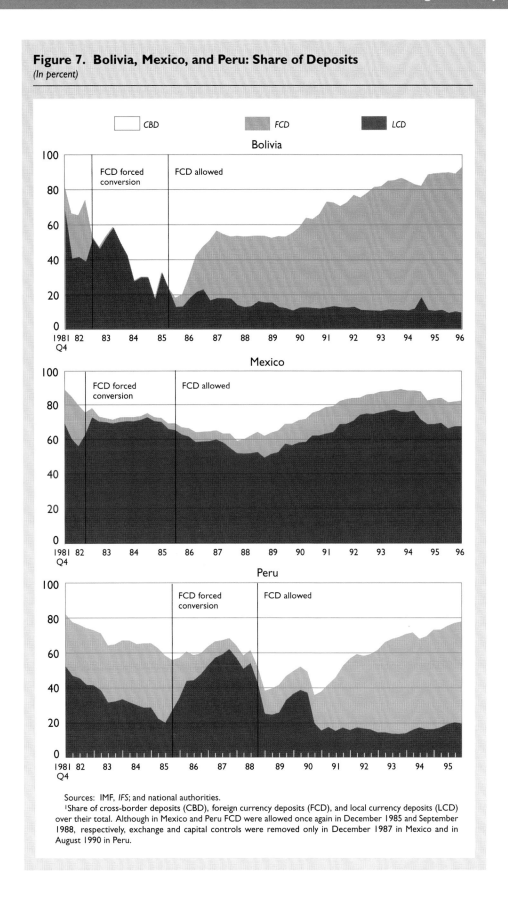

Sources: IMF, *IFS*; and national authorities.
[1]Share of cross-border deposits (CBD), foreign currency deposits (FCD), and local currency deposits (LCD) over their total. Although in Mexico and Peru FCD were allowed once again in December 1985 and September 1988, respectively, exchange and capital controls were removed only in December 1987 in Mexico and in August 1990 in Peru.

of banks' total liabilities. While more effective than reserve requirements in limiting FCD, those measures are also likely to be more distortionary. By limiting access to both FCD and CBD, capital account restrictions can, in principle, also be used to limit dollarization. However, the effectiveness of such restrictions is likely to be transitory at best, since domestic residents find ways to circumvent them.[52] Moreover, such restrictions place a heavy burden on a country's administrative capacity.

Policies to Encourage the Use of Local Currency Cash

Countries can also implement legal and institutional measures to encourage the use of domestic cash over foreign cash. In addition to granting legal tender status only to the domestic currency, all public sector transactions, including tax payments, can be required to be effected in local currency. To assist in this regard, home currency cash should be readily available in all denominations.[53] At the same time, commercial banks should be responsible for importing or exporting foreign cash, and foreign cash should not be eligible to comply with reserve requirements on FCD if banks can fulfill that obligation by holding a dollar deposit with the central bank locally.[54] There may also be some scope for widen-

ing the central bank's bid-ask spread.[55] By raising the cost of roundtripping between local currency and foreign currency, a wider spread can discourage the use of foreign currency cash as a temporary store of value.

The authorities could consider a policy mix that seeks to discourage the use of foreign means of payment (cash and sight deposits) for domestic transactions, while allowing the use of foreign currency as a store of value. In particular, direct restrictions on demand deposits would be effective if, as regards such deposits, FCD are closer substitutes to LCD than to CBD. For instance, since 1980 Israel has limited the use of foreign exchange as a means of payment for domestic transactions by imposing a ban on direct transfers of FCD from one local resident to another.[56] This measure was effective because it encouraged the substitution of sight LCD for sight FCD. However, Israel remains a moderately dollarized economy (excluding nonresident deposits). Other measures to discourage the use of foreign currency means of payment, including some forms of taxation (such as a transaction tax on foreign exchange checks and other foreign exchange payments), could discourage their use in a graduated and flexible way.[57]

---

[52]In Poland, for instance, although accounts in domestic currency are not convertible into foreign currency, they may be converted by withdrawing zlotys, converting them to dollars and redepositing them.

[53]For example, in the Lao People's Democratic Republic, the lack of high-denomination notes contributed to promoting the use of U.S. dollars and the Thai baht. Also, introduction of higher-denominated riel notes in March 1995 prompted a significant increase in the demand for domestic currency banknotes.

[54]Many countries already restrict or do not allow the counting of vault cash in fulfillment of reserve requirements because of the

difficulty in monitoring those balances and because those funds are not immediately available for interbank settlement purposes (see Monetary and Exchange Affairs Department, 1995). However, this could be too costly for banks if their required reserves against FCD must be held with an overseas bank.

[55]The spread, of course, would have to be limited so as not to give rise to a multiple-currency practice.

[56]Measures to restrict the use of foreign cash were already in place.

[57]However, to limit disintermediation into cash or deposits abroad, such taxes would need to be small. In Peru, in the late 1980s, a 2 percent transaction tax on both domestic and foreign currency debits encouraged disintermediation because many households and small enterprises resorted to payments in cash.

VII Program Design in the Presence of Dollarization

In light of the principal recommendations from the preceding analysis (Table 5), this section briefly reviews the design of recent IMF-supported programs in countries with dollarized economies. The main findings from an analysis of a sample of IMF programs are that dollarization has had little impact on program design, and that programs have generally not included explicit measures to try to reduce dollarization—on the grounds that it is an inconvenience that will go away once its underlying causes have been corrected. Perhaps because of this, IMF programs have had little impact on the level of dollarization. At the same time, however, the performance of dollarized countries under IMF programs has not been noticeably worse than that of other countries.

The review of past IMF programs in this section focuses on a sample of 12 countries (highlighted in Table 1) selected to provide diversity in regional distribution, stage of development, and initial economic problems. The sample includes (listed starting with the lowest level of FCD to broad money at end-1995, and ending with the highest) Estonia, Pakistan, Jordan, Poland, Hungary, Lao P.D.R., Argentina, Turkey, Cambodia, Peru, Uruguay, and Bolivia. The first five of these countries (where the ratio of FCD to broad money is below 30 percent) comprise moderately dollarized economies. The other seven countries are more highly dollarized economies.

Inconsistencies in programs with regard to the emphasis given to dollarization may, of course, arise for a variety of reasons. Every IMF-supported program is drawn up in the face of a large number of macroeconomic and structural problems, each of which may influence the design of the program, so that in any particular case other factors may have overridden considerations related to dollarization. Because there is no control for these other factors, the comparisons should be viewed as only descriptive.

General Program Design

There is—with the possible exception of Argentina—no evidence that dollarization has influenced the choice of a nominal exchange rate anchor in IMF-supported programs; other considerations (source of exogenous shocks, level of foreign exchange reserves, scope for fiscal adjustment) have instead been given more weight. In Argentina, there is some evidence that dollarization influenced the preference for an exchange rate anchor (Kiguel and Liviatan, 1994).

There is no compelling evidence that programs in dollarized economies have maintained higher levels of international reserves, to allow the central bank to extend its role as lender of last resort to cover banks' dollar portfolios comfortably. There is little difference between average reserve levels of the seven highly dollarized economies and those of the five moderately dollarized economies (Table 6). Both are somewhat higher than the average of all the dollarized economies considered in this study (Table 7), but this larger sample also reveals little difference, either between highly and moderately dollarized economies or between dollarized and nondollarized economies.[58]

Relatively few programs have included explicit measures to reduce dollarization. Such measures have included policies aimed at maintaining interest rate differentials in favor of LCD. Such a policy is especially evident in Poland, where it was the main consideration of interest rate policy. In most of the other countries in the sample, little concern is evident about the level of interest rates, even though in at least one—Turkey—the level of dollarization appears to display sensitivity—albeit weak—to the real rate of return on domestic currency deposits (Figure 8).

Sharply differentiated reserve requirements and discriminatory rates of remuneration on reserve requirements on FCD have been used in two of the countries in the sample—Bolivia and Peru—with the difference between reserve requirements on LCD and FCD reaching over 35 percentage points in Peru (Table 8). However, in other instances (Hungary, Pakistan, and Poland), reserve requirements have

---

[58]IMF staff estimates of ratios of FCD to broad money for 48 countries were not available, and these are assumed to proxy for nondollarized economies.

Table 5. Recommendations for the Design of IMF Programs in the Presence of Dollarization

Item	Policy Recommendation
I. General Program Design	
Choice of nominal anchor or exchange rate regime	Currency substitution provides an additional argument in favor of a fixed exchange rate. However, the general considerations that guide the choice of an exchange rate system, such as the relative incidence of real versus monetary shocks, are still relevant. Asset substitution tends to increase capital mobility and thereby reduces the scope for independent monetary policy in a fixed exchange rate regime.
Level of official foreign exchange reserves	A higher level should be targeted on account of the greater exposure of dollarized economies to capital flows.
Banking system supervision/regulation	Close attention needs to be paid because of the heightened exposure of banking and financial systems to capital outflows or exchange rate depreciations.
Measures to encourage or discourage dollarization	IMF programs should avoid endorsing measures that discriminate against the use of local currencies. The introduction of institutional constraints on existing dollarization is generally inadvisable.
II. Specification of Performance Criteria	
Intermediate monetary target	If dollarization largely reflects currency substitution, include FCD. If dollarization largely reflects asset substitution, exclude FCD. However, in each case an assessment should be made of the relative stability of different measures of broad money.
Operational target at the level of the central bank or the banking system	As in nondollarized economies, this should depend on the stage of development of the financial system and the availability of indirect monetary instruments to permit the effective control of the chosen aggregate.
Reserve money target	Where intermediate monetary target includes FCDs, include required foreign currency reserves (FCR) in reserve money target. Where intermediate monetary target excludes FCD, exclude FCR.
Treatment of FCR in net foreign assets (NFA)	FCR should be treated as a foreign liability in the definition of NFA to reflect the potentially volatile nature of foreign reserves acquired in this fashion.
Valuation of foreign exchange component of money and credit aggregates	The foreign exchange component of central bank balance sheets should be valued at predetermined (accounting) exchange rates to avoid mechanical and uncalibrated tightening or loosening of monetary policy owing to unanticipated movements in the exchange rate.

been used in a manner that encourages rather than discourages dollarization. In Poland, required reserves on LCD have been markedly higher than those on FCD, at least since 1990. In Hungary, whereas the reserve ratios on LCD and FCD were equal, the de facto treatment of FCD was more favorable because the basis for calculating mandatory reserves on FCD excluded until 1996 banks' FCD at the central bank. In Pakistan, required reserves on FCD were effectively remunerated at higher levels than they were for LCD.

In Lao P.D.R., a decree requiring all domestic transactions to be carried out in monetary assets denominated in local currency was issued. In Cambodia, a similar decree required all government transactions to be denominated in local currency. This has, however, had little effect on the prevalence of currency substitution in the two countries. In addition, the Lao program included measures to promote payments in local currency, with the explicit objective of reducing currency substitution. These have included improvements in payments, clearing, and settlement

Table 6. Some Features of Dollarized Economies

Country	FCD/Broad Money Ratio		Nominal Anchor	Inflation		Velocity		Money Multiplier		Gross Foreign Reserves[1]	
	1990	1995		Average 1991–95	1995	Average 1991–95	1995	Average 1991–95	1995	Average 1991–95	1995
Highly dollarized economies											
Bolivia	70.8	82.3	Money	12.0	10.2	2.7	2.2	4.0	4.6	2.7	5.0
Uruguay	80.1	76.1	Exchange rate	62.3	42.3	1.6	1.9	2.8	2.9	3.0	3.9
Peru	59.9	64.0	Money	113.3	11.1	24.7	29.6	2.5	2.7	8.3	10.2
Cambodia[2]	26.3	56.4	Money	78.8	7.8	12.8	11.1	1.6	1.9	1.3	1.7
Turkey	23.2	46.1	Money	80.4	93.6	3.5	3.0	4.0	4.5	2.9	3.7
Argentina	34.2	43.9	Exchange rate	43.0	3.4	6.5	5.3	3.1	3.6	6.9	7.2
Lao P.D.R.	37.0	42.2	Money	12.4	25.7	9.3	7.2	2.0	2.2	1.5	1.7
Average	47.3	58.7		57.4	27.7	8.7	8.6	2.9	3.2	3.8	4.8
Median	37.0	56.4		62.3	11.1	6.5	5.3	2.8	2.9	2.9	3.9
Moderately dollarized economies											
Hungary	12.2	26.6	Exchange rate	25.3	28.2	2.1	2.4	1.7	1.6	5.4	7.6
Poland	30.4	21.4	Exchange rate	41.7	27.8	2.8	2.8	3.1	3.7	3.2	5.2
Jordan	12.5	15.2	Money	4.3	2.4	0.8	0.9	3.0	3.1	3.5	4.6
Pakistan	2.6	13.6	Money	11.0	12.1	2.4	2.4	2.4	2.5	1.4	3.0
Estonia[3]	23.0	11.4	Exchange rate	55.2	28.9	3.0	3.9	2.2	2.0	2.9	2.3
Average	16.1	17.6		27.5	19.9	2.3	2.5	2.5	2.6	3.3	4.5
Median	12.5	15.2		25.3	27.8	2.4	2.4	2.4	2.5	3.2	4.6

Sources: IMF Staff Country Reports; and IFS.

[1] In months of imports.

[2] First observation for all variables is 1992.

[3] First observations for FCD/broad money, velocity, and money multiplier are 1992; for inflation, 1993.

Table 7. Gross Reserves in Months of Imports of Countries Reporting Information on FCD/Broad Money Ratios

Country	1986	1987	1988	1989	1990	1991	1992	1993	1994	1995
				Highly dollarized economies (FCD/broad money > 30 percent) (18)[1]						
Argentina	**4.7**	**2.5**	**5.3**	**2.6**	**8.0**	**6.2**	**6.5**	**8.0**	**6.7**	**7.2**
Bolivia	**2.3**	**1.3**	**1.5**	**2.4**	**1.8**	**1.1**	**1.6**	**1.9**	**3.7**	**5.0**
Cambodia								0.5	1.6	1.7
Costa Rica	4.7	3.6	4.7	4.3	2.7	4.9	4.2	3.6	3.0	3.2
Croatia								1.3	2.5	2.6
Guinea-Bissau		2.1	2.5	2.8	2.7	2.1	2.1	2.6	2.8	3.0
Lao P.D.R.				**0.1**	**0.1**	**1.4**	**1.6**	**1.6**	**1.1**	**1.7**
Latvia								4.1	4.0	2.8
Mozambique	1.1	1.9	2.4	2.6	2.8	2.8				
Nicaragua		0.2	0.5	2.1	1.9	2.0	1.7	0.8	1.8	1.5
Peru	**4.6**	**1.8**	**1.5**	**2.8**	**3.0**	**6.0**	**6.3**	**7.4**	**11.7**	**10.2**
Turkey	**1.4**	**1.4**	**1.8**	**3.1**	**2.8**	**2.5**	**2.8**	**2.2**	**3.3**	**3.7**
Uruguay	**4.8**	**4.4**	**4.5**	**3.9**	**3.8**	**2.0**	**2.5**	**3.2**	**3.3**	**3.9**
Median	4.6	1.9	2.4	2.7	2.7	2.3	2.5	2.4	3.1	3.1
Average	3.4	2.1	2.8	2.7	3.0	3.1	3.3	3.1	3.8	3.9
				Moderately dollarized economies (FCD/broad money < 30 percent) (34)						
Albania								2.3	3.4	3.5
Armenia								0.7	0.8	1.6
Bulgaria						0.9	2.0	1.3	2.3	2.3
Czech Rep.								2.7	3.9	5.5
Dominica	1.7	2.9	1.7	1.2	1.3	1.7	2.0	1.9	1.4	
Ecuador	3.4	2.2	2.2	2.8	4.2	3.8	3.7	5.1	5.3	3.9
Egypt	1.0	1.5	1.2	1.5	2.3	4.8	9.4	10.1	10.3	11.3
El Salvador	1.7	1.8	1.5	2.0	3.1	2.1	2.6	3.0	2.7	2.5
Estonia							**2.9**	**3.8**	**2.5**	**2.3**
Guinea						0.9	1.1	1.7	1.0	1.0
Honduras	1.2	1.2	0.5	0.2	0.4	1.1	1.9	0.8	1.2	1.7
Hungary	**2.7**	**1.8**	**1.7**	**1.3**	**1.2**	**4.2**	**4.2**	**5.5**	**5.7**	**7.6**
Jamaica	0.9	1.4	1.0	0.6	0.8	0.6	1.7	1.8	3.0	2.2
Jordan	**1.6**	**1.4**	**0.3**	**1.9**	**2.9**	**2.9**	**2.1**	**4.4**	**4.6**	
Lithuania								1.7	2.4	2.3
Macedonia, FYR									1.1	
Malawi	1.0	1.9	3.9	2.8	3.0	2.4	0.6	1.1	0.6	
Mexico	3.1	6.2	1.8	1.8	2.3	3.5	3.1	3.9	0.8	2.5
Moldova									2.9	3.0
Mongolia							0.4	1.7	2.3	2.7
Pakistan	**1.2**	**0.8**	**0.6**	**0.7**	**0.3**	**0.6**	**0.8**	**1.2**	**3.0**	
Philippines	3.5	1.5	1.3	1.4	0.8	2.8	3.1	2.7	2.8	2.3
Poland	**0.6**	**1.4**	**1.6**	**1.7**	**3.6**	**2.4**	**2.7**	**2.4**	**3.1**	**5.2**
Romania	0.8	1.9	1.2	2.5	0.6	1.3	1.5	1.7	3.2	1.8
Russia									0.8	2.2
Sierra Leone	1.1	0.5	0.5	0.2	0.3	0.6	1.1	1.4	1.6	
Slovak Republic								0.6	2.5	3.8
Trinidad and Tobago	3.1	1.5	1.0	2.0	4.1	2.3	1.3	1.7	2.9	2.0
Uganda	0.7	0.9	0.8	0.2	0.8	1.1	1.7	2.5	3.6	3.9
Ukraine									0.4	0.7
Yemen					2.3	3.1	1.3	0.5	1.4	2.9
Zambia	1.2	1.6	1.6	1.1	1.2	2.0				
Median	1.2	1.5	1.2	1.5	1.3	2.1	1.9	1.8	2.5	2.5
Average	1.7	1.8	1.4	1.4	1.9	2.1	2.3	2.5	2.7	3.2

Table 7 (concluded)

Country	1986	1987	1988	1989	1990	1991	1992	1993	1994	1995
Memorandum										
Reserves in 48 countries not reporting FCD/M3 ratios[1]										
Median	2.0	1.8	1.5	1.6	1.7	2.4	2.6	3.2	3.1	2.7
Average	2.4	2.2	2.0	2.1	2.4	3.0	3.1	3.5	4.0	3.6

Source: IMF, *IFS.* Among highly dollarized economies, data were unavailable for Azerbaijan, Belarus, Georgia, São Tomé and Príncipe, and Tajikistan; among moderately dollarized economies, data were unavailable for Uzbekistan and Vietnam.
[1]Classification based on observations for 1995; countries in bold are those selected for review.

procedures; the promotion of the use of checks; and the issuance of large-denomination banknotes.

By contrast, some programs have on occasion accommodated measures that provided incentives for greater dollarization. In Argentina in 1992, for instance, in response to a short-lived run on the currency, the authorities allowed greater scope for dollarization by allowing foreign-currency-denominated checking accounts for domestic transactions, in order to enhance the credibility of the fixed exchange rate regime.

IMF conditionality has only rarely been attached to measures that can be expected to influence dollarization. Perhaps the strongest form of conditionality

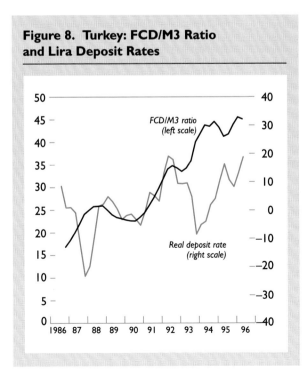

Figure 8. Turkey: FCD/M3 Ratio and Lira Deposit Rates

was in Poland, where failure to maintain a positive interest rate differential in favor of LCD triggered consultations with the IMF. In Lao P.D.R. in 1995, structural benchmarks were set on the removal of floors on the interest rates paid by banks. In Hungary, removal of ceilings on forint deposit interest rates was a structural benchmark under the 1991 IMF Extended Arrangement.

Design of Performance Criteria

For the most part, IMF programs with dollarized economies have adopted relatively standard program targets—performance criteria on the net international reserves (NIR) of the central bank and the net domestic assets (NDA) of either the central bank or the banking system, as well as in some cases indicative targets for reserve money, in addition to performance criteria for fiscal outcomes and external borrowing.[59] The presence of FCD complicates the specification of these targets in a number of ways, which are summarized in the lower panel of Table 5 and are considered in more detail below. Table 9 summarizes how these complications were dealt with in the various countries in the sample.

The first issue a financial program in a dollarized economy must address is whether the intermediate target should be a measure of money including or excluding FCD.[60] The presumption would be that, where dollarization principally reflects asset substitu-

---

[59]Countries with currency boards (Argentina and Estonia in the sample) and countries that use another country's currency (such as Panama, which is outside of the sample) have employed different frameworks.

[60]Of course, as highlighted in Section IV, even measures of money including FCD fail to capture foreign currency cash (especially important under currency substitution) and offshore FCD (especially important under asset substitution).

Table 8. Selected Indicators of Measures Influencing Dollarization

| Country | Dollar-Denominated Bonds | FRR (currency of denomination) | Reserve Requirements (RR)[1] | | Remuneration |
			On local currency deposits (RR)	On FCD (FCR)	
Argentina[2]	Yes	Both	18	18	None.
Bolivia	Yes	Foreign	10	20	Remuneration of RR and FCR introduced in 1991. FCR have generally been remunerated by lower rates than RR.
Estonia[3]	No	Local	10	10	Only excess reserves remunerated, starting July 1996.
Hungary[4]	No	Local	12	12	In 1990–95, average remuneration for FCR was 2 percent, compared with 10 percent for RR.
Jordan	No	Foreign	14	14	Before being equalized in 11/96, FCR were set at 35 percent. These requirements apply to commercial banks.
Lao P.D.R.	No	Local	12	12	Both were remunerated at 1.5 percent.
Pakistan	No	Local	15	15	
Peru	No	Foreign	9	45	
Poland[5]	No	Local	9	4	
Turkey	No	Both	9	10	In the 1991–94 period, RR for liabilities of maturities less than 30 days were 16 percent and for those greater than 30 days 7.5 percent. The respective rates for FCR were 9.5 percent and 11.5 percent. In addition, a further 8 percent for short-term liabilities and 9 percent for long-term liabilities had to be held as reserve in local currency.
Uruguay[3]	Yes	Foreign	20	21.5	RR remunerated at market rates. First 11.5 percent of FCR required to be held in the form of Treasury bills. Balance remunerated at market rates.

Sources: IMF Staff Country Reports; and IMF staff estimates.

[1]Latest available information.

[2]Argentina actually makes use of liquidity ratios rather than reserve requirements. Presently, these are 18 percent for deposits < 90 days; between 90 and 179 days, 13 percent; between 180 days and 365 days, 8 percent; and 0 percent for deposits > 365 days.

[3]Reserve requirements for local currency site deposits indicated. For time HDC of 30–180 days, 14 percent and > 180 days, 12 percent. FRR for time deposit > 180 days drops to 15.5 percent.

[4]RR and RR* have tended to be uniform for much of the 1990–95 period, and averaged just below 15 percent.

[5]Reserve requirements for local currency demand deposits are higher at 20 percent. Before February 1996, rates were 17 percent on HCD and 2 percent on FCD.

tion, the level of FCD is likely to be—barring wealth effects—unrelated to domestic money demand, so that a measure of broad money excluding FCD would constitute the appropriate intermediate target. Conversely, if dollarization largely reflects currency substitution, the level of FCD will be directly related to domestic demand, and a measure of money including FCD would be more appropriate. For the reasons discussed in Section IV, the extent of currency substitution is difficult to assess, and the relative stability

of the different measures of broad money has to be determined on a case-by-case basis.

The programs reviewed did indeed tackle this issue on a case-by-case basis. Of the ten countries in the sample that used standard monitoring frameworks (that is, excluding those with currency boards), seven based their financial programs on a measure of broad money including FCD, implicitly assigning some role to currency substitution. In three of these countries (Cambodia, Lao P.D.R., and

Turkey) there is ample anecdotal evidence of currency substitution. However, in the other four countries there would seem to be a lesser degree of currency substitution, but an intermediate target including FCDs was still chosen.[61] The three remaining countries (Bolivia, Peru, and Uruguay) used a narrower measure of money excluding FCD, owing to a combination of the absence of a stable relationship between broader measures of money and the ultimate policy targets, the perceived inability of the authorities to control such broader aggregates, and an assessment that dollarization was principally caused by asset substitution.[62]

If the intermediate target is a broad aggregate, then a decision must be made whether to apply the operational target at this level—that is, at the level of the banking system—or at the level of the central bank. This decision relates largely to the issue of control and the availability of indirect monetary instruments, as would be the case in a nondollarized economy. Thus, in countries with more market-oriented financial systems (most of the countries in this sample), targets operated at the level of the central bank. In the three countries with financial systems more subject to state control, however, targets operated at the level of the banking system. In Cambodia and Lao P.D.R., credit limits were set at the level of the banking system largely because of the rudimentary stage of development of the banking sector. In Poland, however, the targeting of NDA of the banking system mainly reflected concern about continuing instability in the money multiplier, perhaps not unrelated to dollarization.

For countries setting monetary targets at the level of the central bank, the next question concerns the choice of monetary liabilities that will be subject to targeting. This question relates, in part, to the stability of the money multiplier (the selected measure of reserve money—including or excluding reserves against FCD (FCR)[63]—relative to the chosen inter-mediate target).[64] Once again, this is largely an empirical question. Nonetheless, the usual presumption would be that, if FCD are included as part of the intermediate target, then banks' FCR should be included in the central bank's operating target. Reflecting this, all of the countries in the sample that based their financial programs on a measure of broad money including FCD, except Jordan, established operating targets on a measure of reserve money that included FCR. By contrast, those countries that based their financial programs on a measure of broad money excluding FCD established operating targets on a measure of reserve money that excluded FCR.

Reflecting the decision to treat FCR as a component of reserve money—as a domestic liability—10 of the 12 countries in the sample *excluded* FCR as relevant liabilities in the definition of NIR, although in one of these (Uruguay) this effect is undone by an adjuster. From a purely statistical perspective, FCR are liabilities to residents and should be treated as such in the monetary and balance of payments statistics. However, the operational concept of NIR should be defined differently from the purely statistical concept of net foreign assets (NFA) to provide a more meaningful indicator of the adequacy of a country's reserves.[65] As noted above, treating FCR as domestic rather than foreign liabilities and thus excluding them from the relevant measure of NIR has certain drawbacks. In particular, for the central bank, reserves garnered from FCR are not as secure as reserves gained from intervention or from medium- and long-term borrowing.[66] The two countries that *included* FCR as a relevant liability for NIR were Jordan, on account of the possibility of the introduction of a new currency in the West Bank leading to substantial withdrawals of FCD and thereby of FCR, and Peru, where it was recognized that FCD were subject to the volatility of capital flows and could be withdrawn at any time. Similarly, the adjuster was used in the Uruguay program to ensure that the NIR target was not met simply through the attraction of capital inflows.

---

[61]The inflation experience of these four countries does not suggest that major problems were encountered by targeting the broader monetary aggregate.

[62]These three countries have been able to bring down inflation through controlling the domestic component of money despite prima facie evidence of at least some currency substitution. The exclusion of FCD for Peru is consistent with the central bank's view that domestic aggregates are more appropriate intermediate targets. As noted in Section IV, however, Berg, Borensztein, and Chen (1997) found aggregates including FCD to be better predictors of inflation.

[63]Following Kochhar (1996), a distinction is not made between required and excess reserves, since excess reserves can provide a useful warning of an increase in liquidity and a buildup of potential pressures on inflation, NIR, and the exchange rate. Thus, FCR refers to the sum of required reserves against FCD plus any excess reserves on FCD.

---

[64]The operating target is important not only where explicit indicative targets are set on reserve money, but more generally in the calculation of NDA ceilings at the level of the central bank, since these are derived from a projection of reserve money (together with the NIR target).

[65]This treatment of required reserves is not, however, intended to impugn the virtue of a system of required reserves for FCD, which remains a valuable prudential tool.

[66]An equivalent definition would be to include the foreign exchange assets obtained by the central bank as the counterpart to FCR within "other foreign assets, net" and therefore outside of the NIR concept typically employed for program monitoring purposes. NFA would thereby be unaffected, since they are the sum of NIR and other "foreign assets, net."

Table 9. Selection of Performance Criteria in Sample Countries

Country	IMF Program Type[1]	Intermediate Target[2]	Performance Criteria			Reserve Money		Exchange Rates Used		Treatment of RR on FCD[3]
			Net domestic assets (NDA) Central Banking System	NIR	Definition[3]	Target	Actual	Accounting	
Argentina	SBA, EFF		X	X	CC	No			Domestic liability
Bolivia	ESAF	CC	X	X		No		X	Domestic liability
Cambodia	ESAF	M2X	X[4]	X	BM incl. FCD	No		X	Domestic liability
Estonia	SBA			X		No			Domestic liability
Hungary	SBA	M2X	X	X	CC + TR	No	X[5]	X	Domestic liability
Jordan	EFF	M2X	X	X	CC + DD	Indicative	X		Foreign liability
Lao P.D.R.	ESAF	M2X	X	X	BM incl. FCD	No		X	Domestic liability
Pakistan	SBA/ESAF	M2X	X[6]	X	CC + TR	Indicative		X	Domestic liability
Peru	EFF	M2	X	X	CC	No		X	Foreign liability
Poland	SBA	M2X	X	X[7]	BM incl. FCD	No		X	Domestic liability
Turkey	SBA	M2X	X	X	CC + TR	No		X	Domestic liability
Uruguay	SBA	M1	X	X	CC[8]	No		X	Domestic liability

[1] SBA, Stand-By Arrangement; ESAF, Enhanced Structural Adjustment Facility; EFF, Extended Fund Facility.
[2] M2X includes FCD. CC = currency in circulation, M1 = CC + demand deposits in local currency.
[3] BM = broad money; reserve money definition: CC = currency in circulation; CC + demand deposits, excluding time deposits/CDs.
[4] Performance criteria set on banking system reserves relative to liabilities—essentially prudential requirement.
[5] Accounting rate applied just to items included in NFA; other foreign-currency-denominated components of balance sheet at actual rates.
[6] Indicative target.
[7] At the level of the banking system.
[8] 1996 SBA. SBAs in 1990 and 1992 included total reserves minus reserves of one large state-owned bank.

Finally, it is necessary to decide whether IMF programs in dollarized economies should value the foreign exchange components of balance sheets at predetermined (accounting) or prevailing market exchange rates. This choice is relevant for money targets if there are FCD (for broad money targets) or FCR (for base money targets). If the balance sheet is valued at prevailing market exchange rates, exchange rate depreciations will generate (measured) money expansions if there are FCD or FCR.[67] Valuation at predetermined exchange rates, by contrast, will render money unaffected by exchange rate movements.

The apparent generation of monetary expansions in the context of depreciations could be seen as desirable, in that it would require monetary tightening to ensure compliance with targets. It is not clear, however, that the *degree* of tightening required would be necessarily appropriate. Valuation at prevailing market rates also has the disadvantage that exchange rate volatility close to test dates could make it extremely difficult for the authorities to comply with program targets, despite their best efforts. This would undermine the principle that members should have reasonable assurances that IMF resources will be available if agreed policies are implemented. For these reasons, combined with the availability of reviews for modifying program targets, performance criteria have generally been defined using predetermined exchange rates. In the sample, excluding those countries operating fixed exchange rate regimes, only one country (Hungary) used prevailing market exchange rates in valuing the balance sheet.

Dollarization and Program Performance

The evidence on the effectiveness of inflation control in dollarized economies is mixed. While it seems that highly dollarized economies tend to be associated with higher rates of inflation than other economies (Table 10), the data in Table 6 (for the smaller sample) show little difference between highly and moderately dollarized economies. Moreover, some of the former had fairly low rates of inflation (10 percent or below). Money demand appears to have been more volatile in the highly dollarized economies in the sample, since the coefficient of

variation of velocity is markedly higher than in the moderately and nondollarized samples (Table 11).[68] However, the deviation of inflation from program targets in the first program year, albeit positive, has been only marginally higher than the typical deviation found in the 1994 and 1997 reviews of IMF-supported programs (excluding those countries known to be heavily dollarized; Table 12). Finally, there is little evidence that a higher degree of dollarization implies greater variability in the money multiplier (Table 13), at least when FCD are included in money supply and FCR in reserve money, as is the case for most of the countries in the dollarized sample.

The sample does, however, provide some examples—although not always during the period of IMF programs—of some of the other costs of dollarization. Increased vulnerability of banking systems, particularly in the presence of weak banking supervision, is typified by Turkey, where two banks collapsed in 1994 owing to the impact of exchange rate depreciation on their open foreign exchange positions. Bolivia provides an example where dollarization has generated concern about the central bank's ability to act as a lender of last resort, since a run on banks' FCD cannot be met by printing money. The case of Pakistan, meanwhile, exemplifies the possibilities for misuse of FCD to support inappropriate macroeconomic policies: the central bank requires commercial banks to surrender the counterpart foreign exchange of FCD fully, and the resulting assets have been largely expended.

Overall, countries with IMF programs have not experienced a reduction in the level of dollarization. In 9 of the 12 countries in the sample, the dollarization ratio was higher at end-1995 than at end-1990 (see Table 6). Only in Estonia and Poland did the ratio decline significantly. Uruguay stands out among the highly dollarized economies in having registered some decline in dollarization, but the ratio of FCD to broad money still stands at about 75 percent. In some countries (Bolivia, Peru, and Lao P.D.R.), the dollarization ratio reached a peak in 1993 and has declined modestly since. As noted earlier, however, an increase in (measured) dollarization can reflect a shift onshore of FCD previously held offshore, or indeed merely remonetization, so that successful stabilization and reform may in itself foster an increase in dollarization. The absence of an apparent decline in dollarization is thereby not necessarily evidence of program failure.

On the whole, IMF programs have not sought to tackle dollarization head on. One explanation for

---

[67]Valuation is also relevant for NDA targets if the central bank—or banking system, if this is the level of the operational target—has net exposure in foreign exchange. With market price valuation, exchange rate depreciations will generate NDA expansion (via losses) if there are net foreign exchange liabilities. If there are NFA, on the other hand, it will generate NDA contractions (via profits).

[68]Because of data limitations, the measured velocity includes FCD. But, given that it does not include CBD and DCC, dollarization may be a reason for its higher variability.

Table 10. Inflation in Countries Reporting Information on FCD/Broad Money Ratios

Country	1986	1987	1988	1989	1990	1991	1992	1993	1994	1995
			Highly dollarized economies (FCD/broad money > 30 percent) (18)[1]							
Argentina	90.1	131.3	343.0	3,080.5	2,314.7	171.7	24.9	10.6	4.2	3.4
Azerbaijan							912.6	1,129.7	1,664.4	411.7
Belarus							969.0	1,188.0	2,220.0	709.0
Bolivia	276.3	14.6	16.0	15.2	17.1	21.4	12.1	8.5	7.9	10.2
Cambodia				55.3	141.8	197.0	75.0	114.5	-0.5	7.8
Costa Rica	11.8	16.8	20.8	16.5	19.0	28.7	21.8	9.8	13.5	23.2
Croatia							663.6	1,516.0	97.5	1.6
Georgia	2.0	1.3	0.6	2.0	3.3	78.5	887.4	3,125.4	15,606.5	162.6
Guinea-Bissau	26.5	119.6	60.3	80.8	33.0	57.6	69.4	48.2	15.2	45.4
Lao P.D.R.	35.0	6.1	14.8	59.7	35.7	13.4	9.8	6.3	6.8	25.7
Latvia							951.3	109.1	35.9	25.1
Mozambique	40.5	164.1	58.5	42.1	43.7	33.3	45.1	42.3	63.1	54.4
Nicaragua	681.6	911.9	14,315.8	4,709.3	3,127.5	7,755.3	40.5	20.4	7.7	11.2
Peru	77.9	85.8	667.0	3,398.7	7,481.6	409.5	73.5	48.6	23.7	11.1
São Tomé and Príncipe	13.9	25.0	44.3	42.9	42.2	46.5	33.7	31.8	48.0	64.5
Tajikistan							1,156.7	2,194.9	350.4	610.0
Turkey	34.6	38.8	73.7	63.3	60.3	66.0	70.1	66.1	106.3	93.6
Uruguay	76.4	63.6	62.2	80.4	112.5	101.8	68.5	54.1	44.7	42.3
Median	37.7	51.2	59.4	59.7	43.7	66.0	69.8	51.3	40.3	34.0
Average	113.9	131.6	1,306.4	895.9	1,033.3	690.8	338.0	540.2	1,128.6	128.5
			Moderately dollarized economies (FCD/broad money < 30 percent) (34)							
Albania						35.8	225.2	85.0	22.6	7.8
Armenia							824.5	3,731.8	5,273.4	176.7
Bulgaria	2.7	2.7	2.5	6.4	23.9	338.7	79.4	63.8	121.9	32.9
Czech Republic							11.1	20.8	10.0	9.1
Dominica	2.2	4.7	2.2	6.9	-30.3	5.5	5.5	1.6	0.0	1.3
Ecuador	23.0	29.5	58.2	75.7	48.4	48.8	54.6	45.0	27.3	23.0
Egypt	23.9	25.2	14.2	20.2	21.2	19.5	21.1	11.2	9.0	9.4
El Salvador	31.9	25.3	19.9	17.6	24.0	14.4	11.2	18.5	10.6	10.1
Estonia							1,069.0	89.0	39.8	28.9
Guinea	64.7	36.7	27.4	28.3	19.4	19.6	16.6	7.1	4.2	5.6
Honduras	3.9	2.8	6.6	7.0	21.2	26.0	9.1	10.7	22.5	18.5
Hungary	5.3	8.6	15.7	16.9	29.0	34.2	23.0	22.5	18.8	28.2
Jamaica	24.4	11.2	8.2	16.1	24.8	68.6	57.5	24.5	31.7	21.7
Jordan			6.6	25.7	16.2	8.2	4.0	3.3	3.5	2.4
Lithuania							1,020.5	410.4	72.1	39.5
Macedonia, F.Y.R.							1,692.6	334.5	126.5	16.1
Malawi	14.2	25.1	33.8	12.5	11.9	8.2	23.2	22.8	34.7	83.1
Mexico	86.2	131.8	114.2	20.0	26.7	22.7	15.5	9.8	7.0	35.0
Moldova							1,276.0	788.5	329.6	30.2
Mongolia						20.2	202.6	268.4	87.6	56.8
Pakistan	3.7	4.9	3.3	7.2	9.7	11.8	9.5	9.6	11.8	12.1
Philippines	0.8	3.8	9.1	10.6	12.7	18.7	8.9	7.6	9.0	8.1
Poland	17.8	25.2	60.2	251.1	585.8	70.3	43.0	35.3	32.2	27.8
Romania						5.1	161.1	210.4	256.1	136.7	32.3
Russia							1,353.0	699.8	302.0	190.1
Sierra Leone	80.9	178.7	34.3	60.8	110.9	102.7	65.5	17.6	18.4	29.8
Slovak Republic							10.0	23.0	13.4	9.9
Trinidad and Tobago	7.7	13.4	12.1	4.6	11.0	3.8	6.5	11.1	5.6	5.3
Uganda	215.4	166.7	130.8	45.4	24.5	42.2	30.0	6.5	6.1	7.4
Ukraine							1,209.7	4,734.9	891.0	376.0

Table 10 *(concluded)*

Country	1986	1987	1988	1989	1990	1991	1992	1993	1994	1995
Uzbekistan							645.2	534.0	1,568.0	304.6
Vietnam	487.2	316.7	394.0	35.0	67.0	68.1	17.5	5.2	14.5	12.8
Yemen, Rep. of	13.6	11.4	7.6	13.8	33.5	44.9	50.6	62.3	71.8	48.0
Zambia	54.8	47.6	50.9	123.3	107.0	97.7	165.7	183.3	54.6	34.9
Median	20.4	25.1	15.7	17.6	23.9	30.1	46.8	23.8	25.0	25.4
Average	58.2	53.6	48.2	38.3	54.7	53.8	307.9	369.3	276.1	51.0
Memorandum										
Inflation in 48 countries										
not reporting FCD/M3 ratios										
Median	7.9	7.0	6.3	7.6	7.0	9.1	9.5	8.9	24.8	12.5
Average	13.9	16.5	30.6	70.1	87.7	73.2	296.7	265.2	660.3	63.8

Source: IMF, *World Economic Outlook.*
[1]Classification based on observations for 1995; countries in bold are those selected for review.

Table 11. Velocity in Countries Reporting Information on FCD/Broad Money Ratios

Country	1986	1987	1988	1989	1990	1991	1992	1993	1994	1995	Coefficient of Variation
	Highly dollarized economies (FCD/broad money > 30 percent) (18)										
Argentina	**5.1**	**4.5**	**4.0**	**5.0**	**8.7**	**9.5**	**7.3**	**5.7**	**5.3**	**5.4**	**0.3034**
Bolivia	**10.9**	**6.5**	**5.8**	**5.6**	**4.1**	**3.4**	**2.9**	**2.5**	**2.3**	**2.4**	**0.5802**
Cambodia								**16.2**	**13.4**	**11.1**	**0.1913**
Costa Rica	2.7	2.7	2.3	2.4	2.3	2.3	2.4	2.5	2.5	3.0	0.0856
Guinea-Bissau	5.4	4.1	4.5	6.7	5.8	7.1	6.0	6.7			0.1869
Lao P.D.R.				**10.4**	**13.8**	**14.1**	**11.0**	**7.6**	**6.7**	**7.2**	**0.3053**
Latvia								3.2	2.9	4.3	0.2125
Nicaragua			1.6	2.8	17.5	5.1	5.3	5.1	3.4	2.9	0.9240
Peru	**5.3**	**5.2**	**4.3**	**5.2**	**4.8**	**7.5**	**6.4**	**5.8**	**5.7**	**5.3**	**0.1620**
Turkey		**3.4**	**3.5**	**3.6**	**4.2**	**3.7**	**3.6**	**3.8**	**3.1**		**0.0863**
Uruguay	**1.9**	**2.4**	**2.0**	**1.7**	**1.6**	**1.9**	**2.2**	**2.5**	**2.6**	**2.5**	**0.1640**
Median	5.2	4.1	3.7	5.0	4.8	5.1	5.3	5.1	3.3	4.3	0.1891
Average	5.2	4.1	3.5	4.8	7.0	6.1	5.2	5.6	4.8	4.9	0.2277
	Moderately dollarized economies (FCD/broad money < 30 percent) (34)										
Armenia								2.6	1.0	1.1	0.5646
Czech Rep.								1.3	1.2	1.2	0.0620
Dominica	2.1	1.8	2.1	2.0	1.8	1.7	1.6	1.7	1.7		0.1063
Ecuador	4.9	4.4	4.7	5.8	4.6	4.5	4.6	4.0	3.5	3.3	0.1641
Egypt	1.1	1.1	1.1	1.2	1.2	1.1	1.2	1.2	1.2	1.3	0.0331
El Salvador	3.1	3.5	3.7	3.8	3.3	3.1	2.8	2.6	2.5	2.8	0.1453
Estonia								**3.6**	**3.8**	**4.0**	**0.0538**
Honduras	3.7	3.3	3.2	3.2	3.2	3.5	3.3	3.6	3.5	3.5	0.0580
Hungary	**2.0**	**2.1**	**2.4**	**2.4**	**2.3**	**2.1**	**1.9**	**1.9**	**2.2**		**0.0864**
Jamaica	2.1	2.2	2.0	2.2	2.4	2.3	2.2	2.3	2.1		0.0570
Jordan	**1.0**	**0.9**	**0.9**	**0.8**	**0.9**	**0.7**	**0.8**	**0.8**	**0.9**	**0.9**	**0.1057**
Lithuania									3.9	4.2	0.0551
Malawi	4.5	3.9	4.2	4.9	5.3	5.1	4.8	4.6	4.2	5.4	0.1057
Mexico	3.7	3.7	9.1	5.5	4.2	3.6	3.4	3.6	3.4	3.3	0.4102
Mongolia							1.8	2.9			0.3067

Table 11 *(concluded)*

Country	1986	1987	1988	1989	1990	1991	1992	1993	1994	1995	Coefficient of Variation
Pakistan	**2.3**	**2.2**	**2.4**	**2.6**	**2.6**	**2.6**	**2.4**	**2.2**	**2.2**	**2.3**	**0.0636**
Philippines	3.7	3.7	3.5	3.1	2.9	2.9	2.8	2.4	2.2	2.0	0.2091
Poland	**2.4**	**2.4**	**2.5**	**1.6**	**2.9**	**3.1**	**2.8**	**2.8**	**2.7**	**2.7**	**0.1582**
Romania	2.4			2.0	1.6	2.1	3.2	4.3			0.3955
Russia								4.1	4.7	5.6	0.1648
Sierra Leone	3.5	6.0	5.8	5.4	5.4	6.1	7.8	9.2	9.8	10.7	0.3296
Slovak Republic								1.5	1.5	1.5	0.0086
Trinidad and Tobago	2.1	2.0	2.0	2.0	2.2	2.3	2.5	2.3	2.3		0.0778
Uganda							13.5	10.9	10.4	10.2	0.1366
Ukraine							2.0	3.1	3.7	7.9	0.6169
Zambia	3.2	3.2	3.0	3.3	4.6	4.5					0.2041
Median	2.4	2.8	2.8	2.6	2.9	2.7	2.8	2.6	2.5	3.3	0.1214
Average	2.8	2.9	3.3	3.0	3.0	2.9	3.5	3.3	3.2	3.9	0.1799
Memorandum											
Velocity in 48 countries not reporting FCD/M3 ratios											
Median	3.6	3.6	3.8	3.9	3.7	4.1	3.7	3.6	3.4	4.0	0.1126
Average	4.0	3.9	3.9	3.9	4.1	4.1	4.0	4.0	3.8	4.1	0.1699

Sources: IMF, *World Economic Outlook* and *IFS*. Among highly dollarized economies, data were unavailable for Azerbaijan, Belarus, Croatia, Georgia, Mozambique, and Tajikistan; among moderately dollarized economies, data were unavailable for Albania, Guinea, Macedonia F.Y.R., Moldova, Uzbekistan, Vietnam, and Yemen.

this is that dollarization has not hindered the achievement of other program objectives. Accordingly, it would seem appropriate to continue to apply conditionality in such a way that it "lives with" rather than directly attacks dollarization. In this regard, the selection of intermediate objectives and ultimate targets should continue to be guided by the same criteria as are employed in other IMF programs, although the presence of dollarization means that the selection of the appropriate intermediate monetary target may require a more thorough analysis of its relationship with ultimate targets than usual. Dollarization should also be counted as a relevant factor in the choice of a program's nominal exchange rate anchor.

While the principle of valuing foreign exchange components of balance sheets at predetermined (accounting) exchange rates should be maintained, the practice of excluding FCR from the relevant definition of NIR liabilities should be reconsidered. The application of institutional constraints on existing dollarization is generally inadvisable, given the distortions that may result, but the manner in which, in its absence, dollarization is liberalized should pay due regard to the sequencing of accompanying reforms. With regard to the latter, IMF programs for dollarized economies should attach greater than usual vigilance to banking sector issues, to take account of the additional risks that dollarization poses for banking sector balance sheets.

Table 12. Inflation Target Versus Outcome for the First Program Year in IMF Arrangements

			Deviation[1]
Dollarized sample			
(12 countries, 14 arrangements)			
Average	Target	49.0	21.4
	Outturn	70.4	
Median	Target	14.2	5.4
	Outturn	19.6	
Highly dollarized countries			
(7 countries, 8 arrangements)			
Average	Target	21.8	9.5
	Outturn	31.3	
Median	Target	9.1	6.2
	Outturn	15.3	
Moderately dollarized countries			
(5 countries, 6 arrangements)			
Average	Target	85.3	37.3
	Outturn	122.6	
Median	Target	21.0	4.0
	Outturn	25.0	
1997 ESAF Review			
(31 countries, 58 arrangements)[2]			
Average	Target	20.5	7.0
	Outturn	27.5	
Median	Target	10.1	2.9
	Outturn	13.0	
1994 Conditionality Review			
(29 countries, 29 arrangements)[2]			
Average	Target	54.3	25.3
	Outturn	79.6	
Median	Target	18.0	3.2
	Outturn	21.2	

Source: IMF Staff Country Reports.

[1]Outturn less target.

[2]Excluding countries where the ratio of FCD/broad money is known to be > 30 percent. For the 4 ESAF countries in the sample (Bolivia, Cambodia, Lao P.D.R., and Pakistan), the average and median deviations were 4.7 and 4.8 percent, respectively. For the 8 SBA/EFF countries in the sample (Argentina, Estonia, Hungary, Jordan, Peru, Poland, Turkey, and Uruguay), the average and median deviations were 30.6 and 6.0, respectively.

Table 13. Money Multiplier[1]

Country	1986	1987	1988	1989	1990	1991	1992	1993	1994	1995	Coefficient of Variation
			Highly dollarized economies (FCD/broad money > 30 percent)								
Argentina	2.8	3.8	4.0	1.2	2.2	2.4	2.8	3.0	3.3	3.8	0.2877
Azerbaijan							3.1	2.0	3.2	1.4	0.3593
Bolivia	2.2	3.0	2.3	2.2	2.7	3.1	4.0	4.0	4.8	4.2	0.2871
Cambodia								1.5	1.6	2.1	0.1872
Costa Rica	2.2	2.2	2.1	2.1	2.2	1.8	2.0	2.1	1.9	1.7	0.0804
Croatia								3.7	4.5		0.1445
Guinea-Bissau	1.0	1.3	1.2	1.3	1.7	1.0	1.3	1.4	1.5	1.7	0.1773
Lao P.D.R.						2.0	2.1	2.1	2.2	2.3	0.0649
Nicaragua			1.8	1.9	1.4	1.6	1.9	2.2	2.4	2.5	
Peru	1.6	1.6	1.7	2.3	1.9	2.4	2.3	2.5	2.7	2.6	0.1831
Turkey	3.2	3.2	3.0	2.9	3.3	4.0	4.0	3.9	4.4	5.0	0.1797
Uruguay	3.0	2.6	2.8	2.9	2.6	2.8	2.9	2.7	2.8	3.1	0.0592
Median											0.1797
Average											0.1827
			Moderately dollarized economies (FCD/broad money < 30 percent)								
Armenia							2.4	1.7	1.7	2.0	0.1723
Bulgaria						3.5	3.4	4.4	4.9	4.5	0.1589
Czech Rep.								4.2	3.8	2.6	0.2468
Dominica	3.2	2.8	3.4	4.1	3.8	4.0	4.5	4.6	5.3	5.5	0.2089
Ecuador	2.6	2.7	2.5	2.4	2.7	3.0	2.8	2.8	3.7	4.3	0.2102
Egypt	2.1	2.4	2.8	3.0	3.0	3.0	3.3	3.1	3.1	3.1	0.1281
El Salvador	3.0	2.6	2.5	2.5	2.6	2.6	3.0	2.6	2.7	2.6	0.0672
Estonia								1.6	1.9	2.0	0.1206
Guinea						1.4	1.6	1.6	1.7	1.7	0.0795
Honduras	4.1	4.0	4.0	3.7	3.6	3.9	3.3	3.4	3.0	3.1	0.1067
Hungary	1.5	1.9	2.0	2.0	1.7	1.5	1.7	1.8	1.7	1.6	0.1074
Jamaica	2.9	2.8	2.7	2.3	2.4	2.9	2.7	2.5	2.6	2.7	0.0717
Jordan	2.9	3.0	2.8	2.6	2.5	3.0	3.0	2.8	3.0	3.1	0.0678
Lithuania									2.4	2.3	0.0403
Malawi	1.7	1.5	1.6	1.9	2.6	2.6	2.6	2.2	2.1	1.8	0.2011
Mexico	2.5	3.7	2.1	4.1	5.3	6.2	6.6	6.9	6.9	6.9	0.3702
Moldova							2.4	1.7	1.4	1.4	1.6	0.2314
Mongolia							5.0	3.1	3.4	3.0	3.0	0.2392
Pakistan	2.6	2.5	2.5	2.3	2.2	2.0	2.4	2.5	2.5	2.4	0.0759
Philippines	3.1	3.1	3.3	3.1	3.2	3.2	3.2	3.4	4.0	4.3	0.1216
Poland	2.2	2.9	2.0	2.2	2.2	2.4	2.8	3.5	3.9	3.7	0.2482
Romania				1.6	2.2	3.5	5.1	7.8	3.5	4.5	0.5088
Russia								1.8	2.1	2.1	0.0976
Sierra Leone	1.6	1.6	1.4	1.4	1.4	1.5	1.7	2.0	1.8	1.9	0.1362
Slovak Republic								6.4	6.1	4.6	0.1706
Yemen						1.1	1.1	1.1	1.1	1.1	1.4	0.0970
Median											0.1321
Average											0.1648
Memorandum											
Money multiplier in 48 countries not reporting FCD/M3 ratios[1]											
Median	2.4	2.4	2.5	2.2	2.4	2.3	2.2	2.4	2.3	2.2	0.1875
Average	2.5	2.4	2.5	2.4	2.3	2.2	2.3	2.4	2.3	2.3	0.2217

Source: IMF, *IFS*. Among highly dollarized economies, data were unavailable for Belarus, Georgia, Latvia, Mozambique, São Tomé and Príncipe, and Tajikistan; among moderately dollarized economies, data were unavailable for Albania, Macedonia F.Y.R., Trinidad and Tobago, Uganda, Ukraine, Uzbekistan, Vietnam, and Zambia.

[1] Broad money/reserve money.

VIII Conclusions

Dollarization comprises various financial assets and motivations. In part, it is a result of increased integration of capital markets with the rest of the world, but it may also represent a flight from domestic money in times of high inflation. While dollarization is important in its own right, it is but one of the many consequences that result from these underlying factors. The benefits of dollarization—most generally the greater integration of the economy with international markets and the deepening of domestic intermediation—largely follow from an increased openness of capital markets. The risks, especially the exposure of the banking and financial systems to potential foreign exchange crises, are also linked to more open capital accounts. Thus, the considerations that apply to integration with international capital markets, such as the need for proper sequencing of reforms and, particularly, the impor-

tance of a sound financial market environment, apply a fortiori to dollarization. Dollarization can aggravate the usual problems in these circumstances, including the instability of money demand and of the exchange rate under flexible exchange rates.

Most of the considerations that apply to dollarization in the design of IMF programs really concern the underlying macroeconomic causes, and IMF programs have not for the most part contained specific measures to deal with dollarization in itself. But substantial dollarization does necessitate special attention to certain areas, in particular in dealing with less stable monetary aggregates in assessing the potential advantages—in certain circumstances—of exchange rate targeting in inflation stabilization, and in considering the need to monitor carefully the vulnerability of the banking and foreign exchange markets.

References

Agénor, Pierre-Richard, and Mohsin S. Khan, 1996, "Foreign Currency Deposits and the Demand for Money in Developing Countries," *Journal of Development Economics,* Vol. 50, pp. 101–18.

Baliño, Tomás J.T., Charles Enoch, Alain Ize,Veerathai Santiprabhob, and Peter Stella, 1997, *Currency Board Arrangements: Issues, Experiences, and Implications for IMF-Supported Programs,* Occasional Paper 151 (Washington, D.C.: IMF).

Berg, Andrew, Eduardo Borensztein, and Zhaohui Chen, 1997, "Dollarization, Exchange Rates, and Monetary Policy" (unpublished; Washington: IMF).

Bordo, M., and E. Choudri, 1982, "Currency Substitution and Demand for Money: Some Empirical Evidence for Canada," *Journal of Money, Credit and Banking,* Vol. 14, pp. 48–57.

Calvo, Guillermo, and Carlos Végh, 1992, "Currency Substitution in Developing Countries: An Introduction," *Revista de Análisis Económico,* Vol. 7, pp. 3–28.

———, 1996, "From Currency Substitution to Dollarization and Beyond: Analytical and Policy Issues," in Guillermo Calvo, *Money, Exchange Rates, and Output* (Cambridge, Massachusetts: MIT Press), pp. 153–75.

Clements, Benedict, and Gerard Schwartz, 1993, "Currency Substitution: The Recent Experience of Bolivia," *World Development,* Vol. 21, pp. 1883–93.

Cuddington, J., 1983, "Currency Substitutability, Capital Mobility and Money Demand," *Journal of International Money and Finance,* Vol. 2, pp. 111–33.

Drazen, Allen, and Paul R. Masson, 1994, "Credibility of Policies Versus Credibility of Policymakers," *Quarterly Journal of Economics,* Vol. 109, pp. 735–54.

El-Erian, Mohamed, 1988, "Currency Substitution in Egypt and the Yemen Arab Republic: A Comparative Quantitative Analysis," *Staff Papers,* IMF, Vol. 35, pp. 85–103.

Estrella, Arturo, and Frederic Mishkin, 1996, "Is There a Role for Monetary Aggregates in the Conduct of Monetary Policy?" NBER Working Paper 5845 (Cambridge, Massachusetts: National Bureau of Economic Research).

Feldstein, Martin, and James H. Stock, 1994, "The Use of Monetary Aggregates to Target Nominal GDP," in N. Gregory Mankiw, ed., *Monetary Policy* (Chicago: University of Chicago Press).

Fischer, Stanley, 1982, "Seignorage and the Case for a National Money," *Journal of Political Economy,* Vol. 90, pp. 295–313.

Friedman, Benjamin M., and Kenneth N. Kuttner, 1996, "A Price Target for U.S. Monetary Policy? Lessons from the Experience with Money Growth Targets," *Brookings Papers on Economic Activity: 1,* 1996, pp. 77–125.

Garber, Peter, 1996, "Managing Risks to Financial Markets from Volatile Capital Flows: The Role of Prudential Regulation," *International Journal of Finance and Economics,* Vol. 1, pp. 183–95.

García, Márcio, 1996, "Avoiding Some Costs of Inflation and Crawling Toward Hyperinflation: The Case of the Brazilian Domestic Currency Substitute," *Journal of Development Economics,* Vol. 51, pp. 139–59.

García-Herrero, Alicia, 1997, "Banking Crisis in Latin America in the 1990s: Lessons from Argentina, Paraguay, and Venezuela," Working Paper 97/140 (Washington: IMF).

Giovannini, Alberto and Bart Turtelboom, 1994, "Currency Substitution," in F. van der Ploeg, ed., *Handbook of International Macroeconomics* (Cambridge, Massachusetts: Blackwell).

Girton, Lance, and Don Roper, 1981, "Theory and Implications of Currency Substitution," *Journal of Money, Credit and Banking,* Vol. 13, pp. 12–30.

Guidotti, Pablo, and Carlos Rodríguez, 1992, "Dollarization in Latin America: Gresham's Law in Reverse?" *Staff Papers,* IMF, Vol. 39, pp. 518–44.

Gulde, Anne Marie, Jean Claude Nascimento, and Lorena Zamalloa, 1997, "Liquid Asset Ratios and Financial Sector Reform," Working Paper 97/144 (Washington: IMF).

Kamin, Steven, and Neil Ericsson, 1993, "Dollarization in Argentina," International Finance Discussion Papers, No. 460 (Washington: Board of Governors of the Federal Reserve System).

Kiguel, Miguel, and Nissan Liviatan, 1994, "Exchange-Rate-Based Stabilization in Argentina and Chile: A Fresh Look," World Bank Policy Research Working Paper 1318 (Washington: World Bank).

Kochhar, Kalpana, 1996, "The Definition of Reserve Money: Does It Matter for Financial Programs?" Paper on Policy Analysis and Assessment 96/9 (Washington: IMF).

McKinnon, Ronald I., 1996, "Direct and Indirect Concepts of International Currency Substitution" in Paul Mizen and Eric J. Pentecost, eds., *The Macroeconomics of International Currencies: Theory, Policy, and Evidence* (Gloucestershire, U.K.: Edward Elgar), pp. 44–59.

Miles, M.A., 1978, "Currency Substitution, Flexible Exchange Rates, and Monetary Independence," *American Economic Review,* Vol. 68, pp. 428–36.

Monetary and Exchange Affairs Department, IMF, 1995, "Reserve Requirements on Foreign Currency Deposits," MAE Operational Paper 95/1 (Washington).

Mueller, Johannes, 1994, "Dollarization in Lebanon," Working Paper 94/129 (Washington: IMF).

Obstfeld, Maurice, and Kenneth Rogoff, 1996, *Foundations of International Macroeconomics* (Cambridge, Massachusetts: MIT Press).

Porter, Richard, and Ruth Judson, 1996, "The Location of U.S. Currency: How Much Is Abroad?" *Federal Reserve Bulletin,* Vol. 82, pp. 883–903.

Sahay, Ratna, and Carlos A. Végh, 1996, "Dollarization in Transition Economies: Evidence and Policy Implications," in Paul Mizen and Eric J. Pentecost, eds., *The Macroeconomics of International Currencies*: *Theory, Policy, and Evidence* (Gloucestershire, U.K.: Edward Elgar), pp. 195–224.

Savastano, M. A., 1992, "The Pattern of Currency Substitution in Latin America: An Overview," *Revista de Análisis Económico,* Vol. 7, pp. 29–72.

———— , 1996, "Dollarization in Latin America: Recent Evidence and Policy Issues," in Paul Mizen and Eric J. Pentecost, eds., *The Macroeconomics of International Currencies*: *Theory, Policy, and Evidence* (Gloucestershire, U.K.: Edward Elgar), pp. 225–55.

Recent Occasional Papers of the International Monetary Fund

171. Monetary Policy in Dollarized Economies, by a staff team led by Tomás Baliño, Adam Bennett, and Eduardo Borensztein and comprising Andrew Berg, Zhaohui Chen, Alain Ize, David O. Robinson, Abebe Aemro Selassie, and Lorena Zamalloa. 1999.

170. The West African Economic and Monetary Union: Recent Developments and Policy Issues, by a staff team led by Ernesto Hernández-Catá and comprising Christian A. François, Paul Masson, Pascal Bouvier, Patrick Peroz, Dominique Desruelle, and Athanasios Vamvakidis. 1998.

169. Financial Sector Development in Sub-Saharan African Countries, by Hassanali Mehran, Piero Ugolini, Jean Phillipe Briffaux, George Iden, Tonny Lybek, Stephen Swaray, and Peter Hayward. 1998.

168. Exit Strategies: Policy Options for Countries Seeking Greater Exchange Rate Flexibility, by a staff team led by Barry Eichengreen and Paul Masson with Hugh Bredenkamp, Barry Johnston, Javier Hamann, Esteban Jadresic, and Inci Ötker. 1998.

167. Exchange Rate Assessment: Extensions of the Macroeconomic Balance Approach, edited by Peter Isard and Hamid Faruqee. 1998.

166. Hedge Funds and Financial Market Dynamics, by a staff team led by Barry Eichengreen and Donald Mathieson with Bankim Chadha, Anne Jansen, Laura Kodres, and Sunil Sharma. 1998.

165. Algeria: Stabilization and Transition to the Market, by Karim Nashashibi, Patricia Alonso-Gamo, Stefania Bazzoni, Alain Féler, Nicole Laframboise, and Sebastian Paris Horvitz. 1998.

164. MULTIMOD Mark III: The Core Dynamic and Steady-State Model, by Douglas Laxton, Peter Isard, Hamid Faruqee, Eswar Prasad, and Bart Turtelboom. 1998.

163. Egypt: Beyond Stabilization, Toward a Dynamic Market Economy, by a staff team led by Howard Handy. 1998.

162. Fiscal Policy Rules, by George Kopits and Steven Symansky. 1998.

161. The Nordic Banking Crises: Pitfalls in Financial Liberalization? by Burkhard Dress and Ceyla Pazarbaşıoğlu. 1998.

160. Fiscal Reform in Low-Income Countries: Experience Under IMF-Supported Programs, by a staff team led by George T. Abed and comprising Liam Ebrill, Sanjeev Gupta, Benedict Clements, Ronald McMorran, Anthony Pellechio, Jerald Schiff, and Marijn Verhoeven. 1998.

159. Hungary: Economic Policies for Sustainable Growth, by Carlo Cottarelli, Thomas Krueger, Reza Moghadam, Perry Perone, Edgardo Ruggiero, and Rachel van Elkan. 1998.

158. Transparency in Government Operations, by George Kopits and Jon Craig. 1998.

157. Central Bank Reforms in the Baltics, Russia, and the Other Countries of the Former Soviet Union, by a staff team led by Malcolm Knight and comprising Susana Almuiña, John Dalton, Inci Otker, Ceyla Pazarbaşıoğlu, Arne B. Petersen, Peter Quirk, Nicholas M. Roberts, Gabriel Sensenbrenner, and Jan Willem van der Vossen. 1997.

156. The ESAF at Ten Years: Economic Adjustment and Reform in Low-Income Countries, by the staff of the International Monetary Fund. 1997.

155. Fiscal Policy Issues During the Transition in Russia, by Augusto Lopez-Claros and Sergei V. Alexashenko. 1998.

154. Credibility Without Rules? Monetary Frameworks in the Post–Bretton Woods Era, by Carlo Cottarelli and Curzio Giannini. 1997.

153. Pension Regimes and Saving, by G.A. Mackenzie, Philip Gerson, and Alfredo Cuevas. 1997.

152. Hong Kong, China: Growth, Structural Change, and Economic Stability During the Transition, by John Dodsworth and Dubravko Mihaljek. 1997.

151. Currency Board Arrangements: Issues and Experiences, by a staff team led by Tomás J.T. Baliño and Charles Enoch. 1997.

150. Kuwait: From Reconstruction to Accumulation for Future Generations, by Nigel Andrew Chalk, Mohamed A. El-Erian, Susan J. Fennell, Alexei P. Kireyev, and John F. Wilson. 1997.

149. The Composition of Fiscal Adjustment and Growth: Lessons from Fiscal Reforms in Eight Economies, by G.A. Mackenzie, David W.H. Orsmond, and Philip R. Gerson. 1997.

148. Nigeria: Experience with Structural Adjustment, by Gary Moser, Scott Rogers, and Reinold van Til, with Robin Kibuka and Inutu Lukonga. 1997.

147. Aging Populations and Public Pension Schemes, by Sheetal K. Chand and Albert Jaeger. 1996.

146. Thailand: The Road to Sustained Growth, by Kalpana Kochhar, Louis Dicks-Mireaux, Balazs Horvath, Mauro Mecagni, Erik Offerdal, and Jianping Zhou. 1996.

145. Exchange Rate Movements and Their Impact on Trade and Investment in the APEC Region, by Takatoshi Ito, Peter Isard, Steven Symansky, and Tamim Bayoumi. 1996.

144. National Bank of Poland: The Road to Indirect Instruments, by Piero Ugolini. 1996.

143. Adjustment for Growth: The African Experience, by Michael T. Hadjimichael, Michael Nowak, Robert Sharer, and Amor Tahari. 1996.

142. Quasi-Fiscal Operations of Public Financial Institutions, by G.A. Mackenzie and Peter Stella. 1996.

141. Monetary and Exchange System Reforms in China: An Experiment in Gradualism, by Hassanali Mehran, Marc Quintyn, Tom Nordman, and Bernard Laurens. 1996.

140. Government Reform in New Zealand, by Graham C. Scott. 1996.

139. Reinvigorating Growth in Developing Countries: Lessons from Adjustment Policies in Eight Economies, by David Goldsbrough, Sharmini Coorey, Louis Dicks-Mireaux, Balazs Horvath, Kalpana Kochhar, Mauro Mecagni, Erik Offerdal, and Jianping Zhou. 1996.

138. Aftermath of the CFA Franc Devaluation, by Jean A.P. Clément, with Johannes Mueller, Stéphane Cossé, and Jean Le Dem. 1996.

137. The Lao People's Democratic Republic: Systemic Transformation and Adjustment, edited by Ichiro Otani and Chi Do Pham. 1996.

136. Jordan: Strategy for Adjustment and Growth, edited by Edouard Maciejewski and Ahsan Mansur. 1996.

135. Vietnam: Transition to a Market Economy, by John R. Dodsworth, Erich Spitäller, Michael Braulke, Keon Hyok Lee, Kenneth Miranda, Christian Mulder, Hisanobu Shishido, and Krishna Srinivasan. 1996.

134. India: Economic Reform and Growth, by Ajai Chopra, Charles Collyns, Richard Hemming, and Karen Parker with Woosik Chu and Oliver Fratzscher. 1995.

133. Policy Experiences and Issues in the Baltics, Russia, and Other Countries of the Former Soviet Union, edited by Daniel A. Citrin and Ashok K. Lahiri. 1995.

132. Financial Fragilities in Latin America: The 1980s and 1990s, by Liliana Rojas-Suárez and Steven R. Weisbrod. 1995.

131. Capital Account Convertibility: Review of Experience and Implications for IMF Policies, by staff teams headed by Peter J. Quirk and Owen Evans. 1995.

130. Challenges to the Swedish Welfare State, by Desmond Lachman, Adam Bennett, John H. Green, Robert Hagemann, and Ramana Ramaswamy. 1995.

129. IMF Conditionality: Experience Under Stand-By and Extended Arrangements. Part II: Background Papers. Susan Schadler, Editor, with Adam Bennett, Maria Carkovic, Louis Dicks-Mireaux, Mauro Mecagni, James H.J. Morsink, and Miguel A. Savastano. 1995.

128. IMF Conditionality: Experience Under Stand-By and Extended Arrangements. Part I: Key Issues and Findings, by Susan Schadler, Adam Bennett, Maria Carkovic, Louis Dicks-Mireaux, Mauro Mecagni, James H.J. Morsink, and Miguel A. Savastano. 1995.

127. Road Maps of the Transition: The Baltics, the Czech Republic, Hungary, and Russia, by Biswajit Banerjee, Vincent Koen, Thomas Krueger, Mark S. Lutz, Michael Marrese, and Tapio O. Saavalainen. 1995.

126. The Adoption of Indirect Instruments of Monetary Policy, by a staff team headed by William E. Alexander, Tomás J.T. Baliño, and Charles Enoch. 1995.

Note: For information on the title and availability of Occasional Papers not listed, please consult the IMF Publications Catalog or contact IMF Publication Services.